THE
SKOUSEN
BOOK OF
MORE AMAZING
MORMON
WORLD
RECORDS

THE SKOUSEN BOOK OF

MORE AMAZING

MORMON WORLD RECORDS

Paul B. Skousen

CFI
Springville, Utah

ISBN 13: 978-1-59955-060-2

Published by CFI, an imprint of Cedar Fort, Inc., 2373 W. 700 S., Springville, UT 84663
Distributed by Cedar Fort, Inc., www.cedarfort.com

LIBRARY OF CONGRESS CATALOGING-IN-PUBLICATION DATA
   Skousen, Paul B.
    The Skousen Book of Mormon 2008 world records : and other amazing firsts,
   facts and feats / Paul B. Skousen. — [Rev. ed.].
      p. cm.
   Includes indexes.
   ISBN 978-1-59955-060-2 (alk. paper)
   1. Mormons—History—Miscellanea. 2. World records. I. Title.
   BX8638.S46 2008
   289.309—dc22

                    2007052218

Cover design by Nicole Williams
Cover design © 2008 by Lyle Mortimer

Printed in the United States of America

10 9 8 7 6 5 4 3 2 1

Printed on acid-free paper

CONTENTS

WHO HOLDS THE MORMON WORLD RECORDS?

In 2004, the first official book of Mormon World Records was published. It contained more than 1,600 records, firsts, facts, and feats, and became a best-selling title that was enjoyed in all 50 states and from Australia to Europe and Central America. Since then, hundreds of additional records have been submitted—some quirky, some silly, some amazingly difficult, but all of them fantastic. This collection supplements that original record with hundreds of new additions.

If you have a personal best or unique contribution to the world of amazing firsts, facts, or feats, you are invited to complete the form on the following pages, or submit that information to www.mormonworldrecords.com, or mail your submission to

Mormon World Records
2373 W. 700 S
Springville, UT 84663

Within these pages you will find the most fascinating collection of achievements ever by members of The Church of Jesus Christ of Latter-day Saints. And then flip over a few pages and learn how you can challenge an existing Mormon world record or set one of your own to be included in the next edition of Mormon World Records.

FOREWORD

This supplement to the *The Skousen Book of Mormon World Records and other Amazing Firsts, Facts, and Feats* (MWR) is a book of superlatives. Some of the accomplishments stand on their own as records. Others are simply interesting. The timeless declarations of "What e'er thou art, act well thy part," and President Gordon B. Hinckley's promise that the restored Gospel will "help make bad men good and good men better," are demonstrated in the following pages.

Sources. The vast majority of records in this book have already appeared in newspapers and magazines. Unpublished entries were sent to the editors specifically for use in this book.

Accuracy. If you see your name or another's in MWR, please review the information for accuracy. These records are only as correct as the source materials, and the factual information was conveyed only as accurately as could be expected from a couple of thousand midnight type-a-thons by your bleary-eyed and fumble-fingered compiler.

Missing Information. We would like to include the ward and stake of everyone mentioned, and if yours is missing or has changed, we would appreciate you sending that to us for the next edition.

Wrong Information. If you don't belong in this collection, please let us know immediately so we can remove your entry. Please see the submissions/corrections page. If you have a photo for your printed story, or can update the photo we've used, please contact us immediately.

Submitting a Challenge. Submitting materials for the next edition of MWR does not automatically mean they will be used. Materials submitted to the editors become the property of Mormon World Records and will not be acknowledged. If you want your materials returned, please include a self-addressed stamped envelope. We cannot guarantee that you will receive back any submitted materials. If you send a photo but do not want it published, please let us know in writing at the same time. The instructions on the following pages provide more information.

About These Claims . . . If a record is or was a world record, we indicate that by putting the year and "World Record" in the entry's title. Please note that such records may not be world records today but were indeed world records at the time they were accomplished. Also, some LDS-specific records are only declared as such within the membership of the LDS Church. For example, the longest home-teaching route or fastest mile run by a Mormon. This book and its contents are in no way endorsed by The Church of Jesus Christ of Latter-day Saints, its leadership, or members. Submissions may be e-mailed to records@mormonworldrecords.com, or mailed to Mormon World Records, 2373 W. 700 S., Springville, UT 84663.

PREFACE

It has been pure joy meeting so many new friends whose personal achievements lift them above the average and into the realms of the super achievers! This latest collection includes new material submitted since the publication of the first book in 2004, and a half dozen or so important corrections to fix some erroneous information included in the first volume.

Paul Skousen
March 2008

"HEY, THAT'S NOT RIGHT!"

A book of achievements is a work in progress. The volume of material from which *Mormon World Records* has been mined is massive and ever changing—mistakes happen.

If you see errors or can challenge existing records or firsts in this collection, you are invited to turn to the following pages for instructions on how to submit corrections or your own record or amazing tidbit. Submitting material does not guarantee inclusion in a future book.

IS IT A RECORD?

To be a record, an event, or accomplishment must be comparable and measurable so that others can challenge it. Until a challenger can prove he or she has beaten or improved upon a record in this book, the old record will stand. Interesting accomplishments and events that seem out of the ordinary do not quality as "records" by themselves.

If the accomplishment is not comparable or measurable, for example the first couple wed in the rebuilt Nauvoo Temple or the first Mormon in space, then such events fall into the category of being an amazing first, fact, or feat.

RULES

The performer must be, or have been, a member of the LDS Church (level of activity is not asked for). Any artifact submitted must have a clear connection to the LDS Church, and should be documented. Marathon events are allowed one 5-minute rest period after each 60-minute interval, or 20 minutes rest after every four hours, and 90 minutes rest after each 24 hours of a 48-hour or longer event. A signed log book must be provided to prove constant observation during the course of the activity. If an official organization sponsors the event, that organization should be involved in validating and ratifying the record. Submission of a record-breaking attempt must be corroborated by independent sources (newspapers, adult witnesses, coverage by the media, official representatives of organizations, and so forth). The sole responsibility of the editors is to correct and update information in a subsequent edition. For endeavors where variables might complicate the duplication of a record attempt, please contact us for help with laying down ground rules.

We will not publicize any activity that is or could be injurious to yourself, others, property, or living things. Activities deemed by the judges to be reckless, illegal, or contrary to LDS Church standards will not be considered for publication.

Questions? Contact us at www.mormonworldrecords.com.

CHALLENGING OR SUBMITTING A RECORD

(Photocopy this page or use separate sheets of paper and send to the address on the next page, or submit via the Internet at www.mormonworldrecords.com)

Follow the instructions on this page to:
Challenge or correct an existing entry in this book.
Submit a new record, first, fact, or amazing feat, or suggest a new category.

1. Description of record first, fact, feat: (Use extra sheets as necessary):

2. The Challenger: Who achieved this record (or first, fact, or amazing feat)?
   Name:
   Date of birth:
   Church affiliation: Member/Former Member/Ethnic Mormon (raised LDS but never baptized)/Other (explain): Home Church Unit (Ward/Area/etc.); OR home city and state/province, country:
   Is the Challenger still living? If so, please provide contact information:
   Mailing address:
   Phone number:
   E-mail address:

3. The Source: If you are submitting this information for or about somebody else, how can we reach you?
   Name:
   Mailing address:
   Phone number:
   E-mail address:

What is your association with the person who set the new record? (Relative, quorum leader, etc.):

4. **Proof:**
   a. Witnesses: A list of responsible witnesses' names and contact information.
   b. Log books (if applicable): A photocopy of log books used to record the event.
   c. Testimonials/Documents: Copies of newspaper clippings and/or letters from ecclesiastical/school/Seminary/mission/business or community leader, and/or other documents validating the record.
   d. Photos (optional but always encouraged): If no photos were taken of the event, any photo of the participants is requested but not mandatory. Any format is acceptable (electronic, print, negative, slide, video, clipping, etc.).

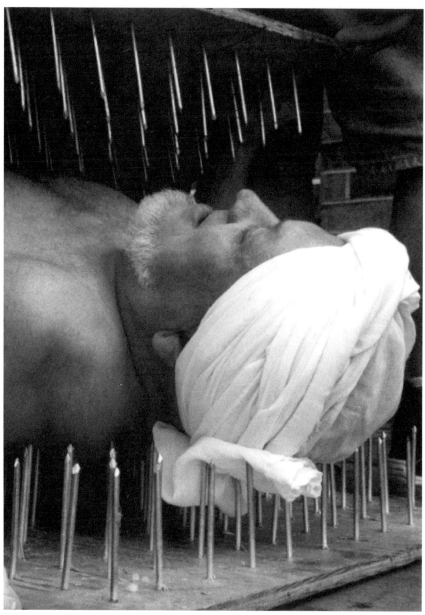

ANDREW J. TONN, *DAILY RECORD*, WOOSTER, OHIO

Vernon Craig demonstrates his unique ability to rest upon a bed of nails—not just beneath, but on top of him too. He invites a few in the audience to sit atop the board and perhaps jump. Such boards are made onsite. "I can't very well carry them on the plane," he says. Brother Craig can also walk through coals 1200–1400 degrees Fahrenheit without a single burn. "It's learning to control your body," he says. No small feat when sandwiched between nails or strolling through the barbecue.

ACHIEVEMENTS

MORMON ACHIEVEMENTS BY THE NUMBERS

.24—Seconds to draw a gun from a holster and fire

1,290—Eggs balanced on end in 8 hours

72,395—Feet high in a balloon

43,252,003,274,489,856,000—Configurations for Rubik's Cube that can be solved by a Mormon in 14 seconds.

FEATURED RECORD HOLDER. Vernon Craig, AKA "The Amazing Komar." Vernon Craig is one of those great spirits in the Church whose appreciation for his many blessings radiates from a warm smile, a gentle handshake, and a soft welcome in his eyes. He was a child of the Depression and grew up in an abusive and poverty-filled environment that built into him an undying appreciation for good health, strong family, and loyal friends.

His assortment of life experiences include being a cheese maker in Ohio's Amish country, a horticulturist at the College of Wooster, and a volunteer at the Apple Creek Ohio State Hospital, where he helped mentally handicapped patients. He was invited on several occasions to give lectures about his work in the mental health field to hospital staff and doctors. He also started the first workable Cub Scout pack in a mental institution. He later worked with Senator Ted Kennedy and others to set up the Special Olympics. During these years, Brother Craig married Ruth, and together they raised a family of two girls and a boy. Sister Craig passed away in 2000.

Brother Craig also became expert at two eastern-Indian skills we don't see much anymore: he could walk on fire and lay on a bed of nails.

The bed of nails is designed with the nails far enough apart (2 inches) so they won't pierce the skin. He let others build the bed of nails because he couldn't carry them on a plane, and he insisted tiny holes be drilled for each nail so they wouldn't be dulled by being pounded through a board. Brother Craig learned to carefully focus and relax, allowing his skin to become supple and pliant, and when he laid on the nails, his skin would yield just enough so it didn't puncture. This wasn't always the case, however, as could be seen in some photos where after the event, a few small trickles of blood from a few puncture wounds could be seen on his back or stomach. He later invented what he called the Iron Maiden, a sort of sandwich of two nail beds, one atop the other, pointed at each other, with

1

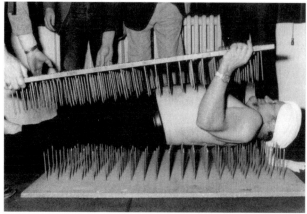

VERNON CRAIG

Vernon Craig asks sponsors to drill holes through the boards before pounding in the nails so they don't become dulled. "Yes, I do get a few minor punctures sometimes," he says, "but that's part of the job."

him in between. Once situated in his Iron Maiden, he would allow spectators to sit, stand, or even jump on the top board.

Fire walking wasn't something he could just stand up and do on command. He needed some preparation time. For his world record walk in 1977, he spent a great deal of time by himself—focusing, concentrating, and clearing his mind, while others built the fire and got the coals going. At such events he never let people take flash photography because the flash would break his concentration. The one time that happened, he had to step out of the coals, and attending doctors confirmed he had second- and third-degree burns on his feet as a result. "It's your mind taking complete control of your entire body, and ordering it through the heat," he said. "And when that control is broken or interrupted, you can get hurt." And he did.

As demand for his appearances grew, he decided he needed a stage name. He had always been fascinated by the poetry of Omar Khayyam, but too many other stage magicians were using Omar. He went back to it once more and happened to get a *K* in front, and stumbled on to the

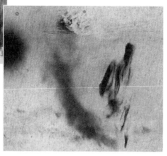

Concentration is key to Brother Craig's fire walking, and the dark of night and no flash photography made that possible. In this blurry, ghostly image he walks across 20 feet of 1,200-degree coals in about 7 seconds.

VERNON CRAIG

name by which he would become famous, The Amazing Komar!

By retirement at age 71, he had performed or lectured in 100 countries, 49 states (never made it to Alaska), and was on all major networks and most talk shows in the early 1970s, such as *Mike Douglas, To Tell the Truth, What's My Line, 20/20, Tom Snyder, Merv Griffin, David Frost, Mike Douglas*, and *Burt Lancaster*.

VERNON CRAIG

Vernon Craig invited audience members to put more weight on his body, and sometimes placed another nail board above on which they could stand.

Brother Craig liked to tease people about retirement: "I'm going to do my last fire walk in Hell." People would gasp, but he kept his word. Just 20 miles outside of Ann Arbor, Michigan, there is a small town named Hell, and it was there that he did his very last fire walk. "I even had my picture taken by the town sign," he said. "It was raining and sleeting, and tiny icicles were hanging from the sign. I sent copies to friends telling them that Hell had finally frozen over."

Today Brother Craig is happily enjoying life as a grandfather of four and great-grandfather of two, and was recently called to be an instructor in his high priest's group. (Author's interview, 6/8/07)

VERNON CRAIG

Vernon Craig walks across coals averaging 1,494 degrees F— without a burn.

LONGEST FIREWALK (1977 WORLD RECORD). Vernon Craig of the Massillon Ohio Ward, Akron Ohio Stake, set a new world record for fire walking when he strolled across 25 feet of hot coals 6–8 inches deep that measured 1,494 degrees Fahrenheit, in Maidenhead, England, on June 12, 1977. This record remained in the Guinness archive of world records for more than two decades before it was broken. When Guinness did a television special to announce its Guinness World Records Hall of Fame, only six people were part of that first class of inductees—and Brother Craig was among them. Paul McCartney of the Beatles was another. (Author's interview, 2007)

BED OF NAILS (1977 WORLD RECORD). On May 6, 1977, Vernon Craig of the Massillon Ohio Ward, Akron Ohio Stake, laid down on a bed of nails with 253 large 20-penny nails 2 inches apart, pointed upward in an array of 11 x 23 nails. He had placed on top of him an identical board of 253 nails pointed down, and invited audience participants to sit on top. He endured this sandwich of nails long enough to hold up 1,642.5 pounds, setting a new world record. "Your mind is a powerful tool that can even ward off pain, if you ask it to," Brother Craig said. (Author's interview, 2007)

LARGEST

WORLD'S LARGEST SNOWBALL (2006 WORLD RECORD). The winter days can be spectacularly beautiful in Michigan, and it was just such a day on February 5, 2006, when members of the Benton Harbor Ward, Kalamazoo Michigan Stake, set out to make the world's largest snowball. By the end of that chilly but bright afternoon, with three hours of snowballing behind them, the 80 volunteers had created two massive snowballs more than 17 feet around, about 1,800 pounds each. One of the requirements set by the Guinness World Records officials was that the snowball be rolled a full turn at least once. That exercise is to prove the stability of the snowball, and

JOE FRODSHAM

The world's largest snowball had to survive one 360-degree roll to be declared the champion. This 1,800-pound monster survived; its twin split after half a roll.

it caused the larger snowball to break in half. Fortunately the smaller one survived. Its official circumference after the roll was 16 feet 9.5 inches, and 5 feet high—a new world record! Later that year, word came that the ward and volunteers were officially accepted as having set a new world record. Anyone up for the world's largest snowball fight? (Interview with Joe Frodsham, 03/28/05)

JOE FRODSHAM

Instead of building their masterpiece by rolling it across a large snowy field in the traditional way, the ward snowball engineers used buckets and shovels to pile and pack snow on a hard, flat parking lot. They built two in case one split. And as it turned out, one did.

JOE FRODSHAM

Many of the 50 Benton Harbor Ward members, along with their friends and neighbors who participated in the Giant Snowball Project, pose with their finished product.

LARGEST PILLOW FIGHT. On December 4, 2004, the youth attending a multi-stake fireside conducted the world's largest pillow fight for youth ages 13–18. For two minutes straight, 674 kids whomped on each other with pillows at the infield of a local Oceanside, California, high school football field. There was no damage to the kids, the pillows survived, and all had a great time. The youth were from six stakes in the San Diego area: Del Mar, Carlsbad, Escondido South, Escondido, Poway, and Penasquitos. (Adolf Singh, 12/29/04)

ADOLF SINGH

The largest pillow fight in the world concluded when all 674 youth had delivered and received at least one blow by pillow, setting a new world record for youth ages 13–18.

BRENT HALE

This is what 158 pounds of teeth look like!

LARGEST BULL SHARK. When Brent Hales, Greenville Mississippi Branch, and his buddies rented a boat that summer in 2005, they had no idea what adventure was about to splash over the side rail to join them. After trolling for the morning off the coast of Ft. Lauderdale, Florida, the friends put out their last two bait fish and hoped for a sail fish or some game fish to grab hold. Instead, a 158-pound bull shark suddenly hit the bait and raced off with 200 feet of wire while Brent fought the shark, trying to tire it out. But twice the toothy foe took off with hundreds of feet of line, forcing Brent to reel it back in again. After 30 minutes, he finally brought it alongside the boat. When his buddies hooked a line into its tail and hoisted it aboard, the fight began. The shark started twisting and rolling and flipping and snapping at anything within reach, and slithered right between Brent's legs. He scrambled over the back of a chair to safety while his friends wrestled the shark down with poles and gear. Fortunately, no one was injured. And then Brent made an elated call to his wife, Candy, with the exciting news: "Guess what we caught today?" (Author's interview, 3/28/06)

LARGEST WATER WEENIE WATER FIGHT. It's the next best thing to Super Soaker squirt guns: surgical tubing tied at one end and inflated with water to create the so-called water weenie super-duper compressed water cannon! On July 27, 2007, a gathering of 142 youth from the Fort Herriman Utah Stake set a new record for the largest water weenie water fight. A total of 950 linear feet of tubing was used. The youth were divided into two teams and carried the 40-plus-pound tubes draped over their shoulders and wrapped around waists. When the signal was given, the combatants waged water war for 12 minutes. It's hard to say who won because, in the end, everybody was wet! (Spence Beckstead, 11/10/07)

LARGEST PAN LOAF OF BREAD (1987 WORLD RECORD). In 1987, two teachers at Eisenhower Junior High in Taylorsville, Utah, decided to give their eighth and ninth grade students the learning experience of a lifetime. R. Clayton Brough, Taylorsville 27th Ward, Taylorsville Utah North Central Stake, and Chris Moore, Country Park Third Ward, South Jordan Utah Country Park Stake, told their students that if they succeeded in making the world's largest loaf of bread, they'd be rolling in the dough!

With the cooperation of other teachers and 200 volunteer students, the research to make a record-setting mega loaf began in earnest in September 1987. In science class, the students began exploring the fermentation aspects of bread making. In Family and Consumer Science, the students learned about the mechanics of bread making and what role each ingredient played. Word on how large of a loaf was being planned reached the

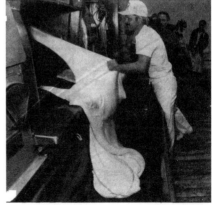

CLAYTON BROUGH

Farmer Jack Bread employees mixed the 350 pounds of dough.

CLAYTON BROUGH

CLAYTON BROUGH

Hercules engineers were anxious to try out their new rocket engine curing oven and happily volunteered the facility to bake the bread. The left photo shows several wires for the temperature probes protruding from the mega loaf.

industrial arts students, who went to work designing and building a bread pan measuring 7 feet long, 2-1/2 feet wide, and 2 feet tall. In the math classes, students puzzled out the proper proportions of ingredients for a loaf this size, also looking hard at the yeast problems because a rising loaf this size could collapse under its own weight. And lastly, helpful businesses donated all the rest. The Farmer Jack Bread Plant helped fine-tune the bread recipe and actually mixed up the dough. The local aerospace company, Hercules, volunteered to cook the bread in their brand new $2 million giant autoclave oven that was installed to bake casings for solid-fuel rocket booster motors. The engineers had not yet fired up the oven and were excited for something to test it with.

The students' goal was to beat the existing world record loaf that was cooked in a charcoal-lined pit in South Africa in 1984, and had measured 4-1/2 feet long and weighed 224 pounds.

Bread Day was November 13. Early that morning, students and teachers converged on the Farmer Jack Bread facility to help mix the ingredients, grease the pan (it took an entire case of the nonstick spray PAM), and knead the 350-pound blob of bread dough that poured from the mixer. Farmer Jack employees treated the kids to donuts and hotdogs, and Coca-Cola provided all the drinks.

The freshly kneaded mega-loaf was placed into an insulated Coca-Cola truck, and with three school buses filled with excited students following behind, the caravan was escorted by two highway patrol cars out to the Hercules oven facility in Magna, Utah.

The Hercules engineers were all ready. They brought out a forklift to move the loaf into the giant 14-foot-tall oven. When its massive door was closed, the clock started. It was 11:30 AM, and the temperature inside started rising. For 2-1/2 hours, students, teachers, engineers, and the media waited patiently.

Meanwhile, the onsite engineers were busy. They had calculated the cooking temperatures mathematically, and were very careful so as not to over-bake the outside of the loaf before the inside was finished. They had put numerous temperature probes throughout the loaf to relay information so they could adjust the oven temperatures as needed.

When the cooking time ended, the door was opened to cheers and applause as the crown

CLAYTON BROUGH

After several hours of cooling, Bill Hennesey of Farmer Jack Breads sawed open the mega loaf to the oh's and ah's of students and engineers alike.

of a nicely toasted loaf could be seen poking above the bread pan. The bread needed another 4 hours to cool, and then a large handsaw was used to cut off the heel, exposing a beautifully and thoroughly cooked loaf of bread. Its official weight was 307 pounds, and it measured 7-feet long, 2 feet 5 inches wide, and 1 foot 8 inches high. The original intent was to donate the finished loaf to the Salvation Army, but cutting it up and bagging it was too cumbersome, so

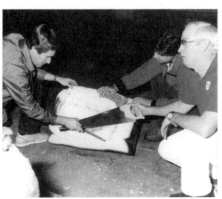

CLAYTON BROUGH

Clayton Brough (left) and Bill Hennesey (right) check out the mega-loaf to see if it cooked all the way through . . . and if so, was it ready for peanut butter and jam?

instead Farmer Jack's donated the equivalent in normal-sized loaves. Meanwhile, all of those involved enjoyed eating most of the mega-loaf themselves, spreading butter and jam on as big a slab of bread as they wanted!

The entire project is estimated to have cost about $50,000 in donated supplies and time, but the experience to the students was priceless. "These many years later," Chris Moore said, "former students still stop me to exclaim what a great learning experience that was." Clayton Brough told the media afterward, "Attempting world records are more than just fun—they also teach important educational skills to students, including creativity, organization, cooperation, communications and logistics." He said his challenge to students everywhere is, "If you want to be successful, then dream big, work hard and pray often!" (Author's interview with Clayton Brough and Chris Moore, 2007; *Deseret News*, 11/14/87; *Salt Lake Tribune*, 11/15/87; *West Valley View*, 11/19/87)

LARGEST GROUP HIKE (MODERN DAYS). Who in the Church can claim the longest large-group hike? To commemorate the original Zion's Camp—a trek started May 4, 1834, with about 200 men and some women and children led by Joseph Smith from Ohio to Missouri—a group of 251 LDS young men and their leaders from various stakes embarked on a tough hike of their own. Members of the Indianapolis North Stake, Bloomington Indiana Stake, Lafayette Indiana Stake, and the Muncie Indiana Stake hiked the longest and most difficult hiking trail in Indiana, beginning on June 20, 2005. The six-day hike on the Knobstone trail led them through nearly 40,000 acres with some 58 miles of back country hiking. In those six days the group hiked 50 miles total, about 3–6 hours per day, depending on the difficulty, and unlike the first Zions Camp, group leaders report there was not one apostasy from among their numbers. (Marc Duerden, 7/4/05)

ADOLF SINGH

Let's see now, doing the locomotion dance appears to be Sister Groucho Marx followed by Sister Groucho Marx and Sister Groucho Marx and Sister Groucho Marx and Sister . . .

LARGEST LOCOMOTION DANCE. A locomotion dance is where people line up behind each other, place hands on the hips of the person in front, and move forward and/or backward in unison. On December 4, 2004, at a multi-stake activity in San Diego, California, 967 youth performed the longest locomotion dance in the Church for 7 minutes. In all, the group traveled halfway around the high school track where the event was staged, stepping to the music for a total of 220 yards. The youth represented local stakes: Del Mar, Carlsbad, Escondido South, Escondido, Poway and Penasquitos. (Adolf Singh, 12/29/04)

LARGEST ROCK, PAPER, SCISSORS TOURNAMENT (2007 WORLD RECORD). The largest tournament of contestants to outwit each other in the ultimate throwdown of hand gestures took place among BYU students on April 7, 2007, at the Deseret Tower field on the BYU campus. A total of 765 people showed up to outwit each other for the grand prize. Each participant received a T-shirt for their $5 entrance fee, and a chance to be listed in the *Guinness Book of World Records*. Congratulations to the winner, 18-year-old Mitch Hayashi, who outlasted them all and won a decorated rock trophy and $2,500. (*Deseret News*, 4/7/07)

WORLD'S LARGEST PUZZLE. Chris and Naomi Hathaway, Pleasant View 2nd Ward, Sharon East Stake, have an amazing knack for puzzling through any sort of problem. But nothing compares to their almost one-year achievement of completing the world's largest commercially-sold puzzle. This dauntingly huge challenge has 18,000 pieces and, when completed, measured 6 feet 3 inches by 9 feet—large enough to replace that Persian rug under your kitchen table. The puzzle is made in Germany by Ravenburger, and puzzlers around the world engage in contests to see who can complete this puzzle the quickest. But finishing that particular puzzle wasn't what Brother Hathaway had in mind when he first started court-

CHRIS HATHAWAY

Never mind the 18,000 pieces perfectly assembled to finish this the world's largest puzzle. It's the two BIG pieces at the top of this photo that got together—*that's* the puzzle everybody was hoping to solve!

ing his wife-to-be. He had served a mission in Austria, where puzzles are quite prevalent. After coming home, he and Naomi began dating, and one evening they found themselves in a game store. Seeing the Ravenburger giant puzzle, Naomi exclaimed she wanted to give that one a try. Chris loved the idea because it would keep the two within arm's length for many long hours at a time. The couple started the puzzle on April 25, 2004, fell in love, and got married in July. They completed the puzzle the following April 17, 2005. Until room is made for its display in their little newlywed apartment, this goliath puzzle is rolled up in two sections and is stored away as proof that with enough searching and selecting, eventually the right puzzle pieces can line up just perfectly. (Author's interview, 11/13/05)

ADOLF SINGH

There were a few sore jaws and hoarse voices, but Christmas was never merrier than when the world carol-singing record was broken and the singing could finally stop!

LARGEST CAROL SERVICE (2004 WORLD RECORD). It wasn't yet Christmas on December 4, 2004, but that didn't stop 1,065 youth of the North County California stakes from setting a world record for the largest Christmas carol service. They sang carols nonstop, in unison, for 28 minutes and 30 seconds, breaking the old record by 30 seconds. (Adolf Singh, 12/29/04)

LARGEST MUSICAL INSTRUMENT ENSEMBLE—FOR UNCONVENTIONAL INSTRUMENTS (2007 WORLD RECORD).

PAUL B. SKOUSEN

Elisabeth Skousen (front, left) shows a cameraman one of the Masonite boards that when loosely flexed with vigor makes the unique woop-woop sound that was delightfully popularized in the 1960 hit "Tie Me Kangaroo Down, Sport."

On November 9, 2007, a most unusual musical ensemble was performed by 487 students at Eisenhower Junior High in Taylorsville, Utah. With a recording of Rolf Harris's 1960 international smash hit, "Tie Me Kangaroo Down, Sport," playing over loud speakers, the students used 2 x 3-foot thin Masonite boards to create the song's unique backdrop wooble sound. The wobble board is played by holding the board on either side and thrusting it forward and backward, allowing it to flex and snap back, giving the unique wobble sound. Performers had to apply tape to their hands to prevent blisters for the 5-minute and 16-second song. Harris's song is about a dying Australian stockman who instructs his friends how to fill his last dying wishes—"tie me kangaroo down, sport," "watch me wallabys feed, mate," "keep me cockatoo cool, Curl," "take me koala back, Jack," "let me Abos go loose, Lou," "Mind me platypus duck, Bill," "Play your digeridoo, Blue," and "tan me hide when I'm dead, Fred." (Author, 11/9/07; Clayton Brough, 11/12/07)

PAUL B. SKOUSEN

A few teachers 487 youth waggle their wobble boards in tune to "Tie Me Kangaroo Down, Sport," breaking the old record by 100 participants.

TALLEST

TALLEST TOWER OF PENCILS (2006 WORLD RECORD). The world's tallest tower of pencils was carefully built by ninth grade students at Eisenhower Junior High in Taylorsville, Utah, on October 20, 2006, under the sponsorship of R. Clayton Brough, Taylorsville 27th Ward, Taylorsville Utah North Central Stake, Tom Sharpe (LDS), and Kelly Huntington. Using 1,943 standard unsharpened pencils, the students' tower rose to 9 feet 6 inches in exactly four hours. Their example inspired other schools to break that record, and as of June 2007, a school in Missouri built a 12-foot tower using 1,308 pencils. (Author's interview, 5/30/07)

CLAYTON BROUGH

TALLEST FREE-STANDING PAPER STACK (2005 WORLD RECORD).
On June 15, 2005, a group of LDS employees at a children's newspaper
company in Lindon, Utah, stacked unfolded newspapers to 10 feet 2 inches
high in just shy of 4 hours. The stack of 39,024 sheets of newsprint stood
unaided for 30 seconds, although it was a wobbly 30 seconds. "Don't try
this at home!" said Debbie Ostler, an employee who helped unfold more
than 50,000 surplus newspapers that were preserved for the event. "We
all thought a stack of newspaper would be pretty solid, but when we got
over six feet, it became almost fluid-like, slipping this way and that, like a
column of Jell-O," she said. When the allotted time expired, the stack was
pushed over and slammed to the cement with a bang! (Author's interview,
6/15/05)

PAUL B. SKOUSEN

How many single pieces of newsprint does it take to make a ten-foot stack?
At least 39,000, according to these intrepid paper stackers. Posing in front of
their world-record stack are (l-r) Paul Skousen, Debbie Ostler, Jessica Seag-
miller, Nanette Suta, Jon Baird, Diane Teahan, Chris Manning, Nick Bowen,
Kristy Glather, TJ Stanley, Greg Morley, Cody Zavala, Ryan Carter, Harold
Skousen, Chris Willis, and Ben Fillmore (not pictured: Susan Starkweather).

TALLEST ICE CREAM CONE (2005 WORLD RECORD). On May 15, 2005,
three ninth-grade students from Eisenhower Junior High School set a new
world record for the tallest ice cream cone with a height of 13.00 inches. Team
member Autumn Jones, who is in her Young Women's group at her Taylorsville, Utah ward, was joined by friends Cassidee Cline and Vanja Knezevic.

Each team had 20 minutes to build the tallest cone possible using only their hands, a standard scoop, and commercially-made chocolate or vanilla ice cream. Sister Jones's job was to load the ice cream into the scoop and hand it off to a friend who stacked it atop a cone held by the third team member. Autumn's team was successful by keeping their column of scoops very balanced and straight. (Author's interview, 5/15/05)

CLAYTON BROUGH

HIGHEST

HIGHEST BALLOON FLIGHT (1935 WORLD RECORD). On November 11, 1935, BYU graduate Captain Orvil A. Anderson and Albert W. Stevens piloted one of history's most remembered balloons ever to ascend into the stratosphere. The massive creation of reinforced rubberized fabric, cables, and a gondola, named *Explorer II*, stood 316 feet high (as tall as a 31-story building) when inflated, and at altitude where low air pressure allowed the helium gas to expand the balloon to a sphere, it held 3,700,000 cubic feet of gas and was more than 190 feet in diameter. This was the largest balloon ever made. Launched at 6:45 AM from South Dakota's famous Stratobowl, the balloon was almost pushed into the surrounding cliffs, but by dropping iron

USAF

Prior to takeoff, *Explorer II* stood taller than a 31-story building. At altitude, the bag expanded into a near sphere of more than 200 feet in diameter.

pellets, it quickly ascended and eventually leveled off its ascent speed to 400 feet per minute. Inside, the two Army Corps officers communicated via radio to the 21,000 visitors who were on hand to watch the historic event. The balloon topped out at 72,395 feet, a new world record. And at this height, the men enjoyed watching the curvature of the earth and the blue disappear into the black of outer space. They had become the world's first astronauts. (Ruth Stevens, "My Husband the First Astronaut," *Improvement Era*, May 1936; various sources)

15

STEVEN ANDERSON

Model rocketry taken to the next level is more than 17,000 feet into the sky.

HIGHEST FLOWN MODEL ROCKET. On August 8, 2004, on Utah's Bonneville Salt Flats, Steven Anderson, Bountiful 7th Ward, Bountiful Utah South Stake, set a world altitude record for model rockets. His 5-foot tall homemade masterpiece blasted to 17,030 feet, a new record for rockets in its class. He used a K660 model rocket motor (that's rocket enthusiast vernacular for a rocket engine consisting of a heavy tube almost 2 inches in diameter and about a foot long, packed with explosive stuff). An onboard altimeter determined the altitude. On its fall to earth, a parachute automatically deployed at 700 feet for a safe landing. (Steven Anderson, 11/11/04)

DEEPEST

DEEPEST DEEP-SEA DIVE—WOMEN (1950 WORLD RECORD). On May 14, 1950, Norma Armour Hanson, Harbor 1st Ward, Palos Verdes California Stake, climbed into her 120-pound diving suit and, smiling for cameras, was lowered into the California coastal ocean to set a new women's deep-sea diving record of 220 feet. The trip down took only 10 minutes, but coming back up took 2 hours and 40 minutes to allow for proper decompression. She was inducted into the Women Divers Hall of Fame for her pioneering work in deep-sea diving. For a more detailed telling of her many exploits, an encounter with a shark, and her Hollywood underwater stunts, see her writeup in the Courage section of this book. (Author's interview, 2/26/05)

NORMA HANSON

Norma Hanson waves good-bye as she prepares to set a new depth record for women deep sea divers. (Photo by Bob Plunkett, Los Angeles, CA.)

FARTHEST

FARTHEST MARSHMALLOW NOSE BLOW. Using regular miniature marshmallows, Gavin Eddy and Mahonri Pacanos, San Diego, California, managed to launch their payloads an equal distance of 13 feet 0 inches on December 4, 2004. This highly athletic event required that the record challenger place the small marshmallow in the nostril of his or her choice. With a finger holding the other nostril closed, a single blast of air from their lungs was all that was allowed to propel the small treat through the air. The two winners were participants at a multi-stake youth activity and out-blew dozens of contestants for this prestigious new Mormon World Record. (Adolf Singh, 12/29/04)

Nothing to sneeze at . . . Mahonri Pacanos blows it for a new Mormon World Record.

ADOLF SINGH

MOST

MOST RECORDS SET BY A SINGLE YOUNG GROUP AT ONE TIME (2004). At a multi-stake youth activity on December 4, 2004 at the El Camino High School football stadium, more than 1,000 youth from the seven LDS stakes in North County, California, gathered for some serious record breaking. By day's end, they had set six new world records and eight new Mormon World Records: farthest marshmallow nose blow; most people in a VW bug; largest nonstop Christmas carol singing; longest locomotion dance; largest group to wear Groucho Marx masks; fastest human conveyor belt; most grapes in mouth; most spoons balanced on face; most tennis balls in hand; loudest scream, burp, and finger snap; largest pillow fight; and fastest time to eat an onion. (All records from event coordinator Adolf Singh and local newspaper coverage.)

ADOLF SINGH

Mark Robles carefully pushes in the last of 60 grapes into his mouth, setting a new world record in 2004. To prove no grapes were squashed, all must be spit out whole and intact.

MOST GRAPES IN THE MOUTH (2004 WORLD RECORD). A new world record was set on December 4, 2004, at a San Diego multi-stake youth activity when Mark Robles stuffed 60 grapes into his mouth in 25 seconds and held it for 10 seconds. The grapes weighed 4.55 ounces, could not be squished or chewed, and had to be spit out whole. The old world record was 54 grapes. (Adolf Singh, 12/29/04)

ADOLF SINGH

MOST PEOPLE IN A VW BUG (2004 WORLD RECORD). At a multi-stake youth activity in San Diego, California, on December 4, 2004, a new world record was set when 31 people were stuffed into a Volkswagen Beetle, shattering the old record of 27. Said one participant, "It was really hot." And another, "I didn't like somebody's dirty socks stuffed in my face." But they all survived just fine! (Adolf Singh, 12/29/04)

ADOLF SINGH

Heads, hands, stinky feet, and claustrophobic feelings aside, these youth set a new record of 31 in a VW Beetle. From the Fallbrook Ward, Vista Stake: Verenice Loza, McKenzi Aledo; from the Valley Center Ward, Escondido Stake: Michael Handy, Kory Hansen, Stina Oakes, Kelsey Merakco, Trenton Meddors; from the Penasquitos 1st, 2nd, and 3rd Wards, Penasquitos Stake: Brett McConnell, Josh Mendenhall, Evan Jones, Parker Welch, Aubrey Barlow, Victoria Winter, Marissa Lang; from the Vista Ward, Vista Stake: Kelsey Payne, Sandra Mendoza, Alex Coleman, Alexis Wilson, Cristina Aguilar, Michael Hansen, Felicia Anderson; from the San Marcos Ward, Escondido Stake: Trevor Knight, Tati Slagle, Erik Porter; from the Carlsbad 1st and 3rd Wards, Carlsbad Stake: Grant Perdue, Daniel Allen, Eric Kennedy; from the Poway Ward, Poway Stake: Spencer Nelson; from the Encinitas Ward, Del Mar Stake: McClain Morris; from the Oceanside 1st Ward, Carlsbad Stake: Dillon McFadden; from the Del Mar Ward, Del Mar Stake: Janelle Baldwin.

MOST SPOONS BAL-ANCED ON FACE. It's not as easy as it looks! At a multi-stake youth activity in San Diego on December 4, 2004, Tyler Talbot, Poway 1st Ward, Poway California Stake, balanced eight spoons on his face while standing upright. (Adolf Singh, 12/29/04)

ADOLF SINGH

In Grandpa's day, spooning meant something completely different than this trick. Tyler Talbot managed to balance eight spoons on his face for a count of ten.

MOST EGGS BALANCED, INDIVIDUAL (2005 WORLD RECORD). On September 21, 2005, former BYU student Brian Spotts set a new world record for egg balancing during a sponsored demonstration in Melbourne, Australia. In 15 hours, Spotts stood up 439 eggs on their ends. Is it hard? Not really, Spotts says. "After a couple of hours it gets pretty easy," he said. "I just get into a groove." Spotts explained that you just "hold the egg with your thumb and your four fingers and lean it until it stands up straight. The trick is patience." (BYU NewsNet, 9/21/05)

BYU NEWSNET

The science and skill of egg balancing is more about patience and a steady hand than it is about movement of celestial orbs around the earth or sun. As Brian Spotts demonstrates in this photo, it's about holding the egg upright while the yoke settles to the bottom. So, what's for breakfast?

MOST EGGS BALANCED, GROUP (2003 WORLD RECORD). It's not eggsactly the kind of thing parents send their kids to college for, and this is no yoke, but for a brief moment of shining glory in 2003, some 100 students at BYU were the world's very best at egg balancing. The trick is to hold a raw egg upright until the yoke settles to the bottom, or at least centers itself. It takes a few seconds, but an egg can indeed be balanced on its fatter end, with enough patience, and will remain standing perfectly upright. Led by fellow student and egg balancing champ Brian Spotts, the students invaded the Garden Court of the Wilkinson Center on March 15, 2003, and in 6-1/2 hours, they balanced 1,290 eggs—a new world record. An important note from this event: There is a myth that when the sun and earth are lined up, an event called the equinox, gravitational forces are so perpendicular to the earth's surface that an egg can be balanced on that day. This is not the case. Eggs can be balanced any day and any time, even when it's hot enough to fry one on the sidewalk. (BYU NewsNet)

JAMIE JACKSON

You might call this "resting on your laurels," but they're actually some of the 35 wedding bouquets caught by Jamie Jackson to set a new world record.

MOST WEDDING BOU-QUETS CAUGHT (2007 WORLD RECORD). Standing a touch over five feet tall, the world champion bouquet catcher with a record of 35 clean catches is Jamie Alisha Jackson, Hidden Valley 5th Ward, Hidden Valley Utah Stake. She smashed the old record of nine many weddings ago. "Don't be shy and bashful when it comes to getting your prize," Sister Jackson says. "When it is thrown, go full bore, but be aware of little children!" In one such event she out-jumped some gals who were close to six-feet tall, and snagged the bouquet right in front of their outstretched hands. "On film, it looked like a football pass with a perfect interception," she said. "It was so hilarious!" Sister Jackson is still awaiting her own bouquet, so pay attention to her, elders—such a talented and all-around wonderful gal won't be on the waiting list much longer (especially when word gets out of her potential as a powerful secret weapon in backyard football games!). (Interview with Jamie Jackson, 6/20/07)

MOST WEDDING GARTERS CAUGHT. As of November 2006, Paul L. Wilson, Hidden Valley 5th Ward, Hidden Valley Utah Stake, has caught 17 garters. The tradition is that during a wedding reception, often near the end, the groom will remove a ceremonial garter from his new bride's leg and since it's elastic, he can flip it into a group of bachelors. Like the wedding bouquet toss, the idea is that whoever catches the garter is

JAMIE JACKSON

Height gives little advantage when snagging those wedding bouquets—it's all about keeping your eye on the fall.

declared the next one to get married. This is why on one occasion Brother Wilson had to really fight for the garter with a 10-year-old. "On principle, I couldn't let him have it," he said. "If the superstition was true, I wasn't about to wait for him to come of age." (Author's interview, 9/10/07)

MOST BALLOONS INFLATED. KC Williams of West Valley, Utah, is an amazing man. He not only set at least three Guinness World Records but donates hundreds of hours and thousands of balloons to fund-raising and awareness events such as walkathons and charity events. During the 2002 Winter Olympics and Paralympics in Salt Lake City, he performed 30 times and blew up an estimated 100,000 balloons. Those balloons are hard to inflate. The 260-Q inflates to 60 inches long and 2 inches in diameter. The 160-Q is terribly difficult and is only one inch in diameter and 60 inches long. Both sizes of balloon come with a warning: "Do

PAUL B. SKOUSEN

KC Williams, the "Balloon Man," donates hundreds of hours and thousands of balloons at fund-raiser events to help bring a little joy to children with life-threatening diseases.

CLAYTON BROUGH

As part of a new world record in 2005, KC Williams inflated more than 1,200 balloons that students at Utah's Eisenhower Junior High in Taylorsville linked together to make the world's longest balloon chain at 708 feet long.

not attempt to inflate by mouth." Among his amazing achievements are these world records:

• **Most 260-Q Balloons Inflated, 1 hour (2003 World Record).** On September 21, 2003, Brother Williams inflated and tied 661 balloons, a new world record. This size is typically used to make poodles, hats, swords, etc. Following this record-setting effort, Williams said his cheek was strained and swollen, and he temporarily lost vision in his left eye. "I hurt for a long time after," he said.

• **Most 160-Q Balloons Inflated, 1 hour (2004 World Record).** On December 4, 2004, Brother Williams inflated and tied 131. Official rules required him to inflate the 160-Q balloons to 18 inches for the record, an effort that left him winded after each blow.

PAUL B. SKOUSEN

The official warning on every package of 260-Q and especially 160-Q balloons is "Do not inflate by mouth." KC Williams said that when he's tired or it's hard to get a balloon started, he'll sometimes wind up like he's kick-starting a motorcycle, thrusting his foot down to explode as much lung energy as possible to get beyond that first hard inflation barrier.

• **Most 160-Q Balloon Animals Shapes (2004 World Record).** On September 19, 2004, Brother Williams set a new world record by inflating, tying, and twisting 89 160-Q balloons into animal shapes in one hour.

• **Most Balloons Inflated in One Minute (2004 World Record).** On December 4, 2004, KC Williams of West Valley, Utah, inflated 13 260-Q balloons in 60 seconds. After a breather he set a second record by inflating four 160-Q balloons in sixty seconds. (Author's interview)

MOST TENNIS BALLS IN ONE HAND.
On December 4, 2004 at a youth activity in San Diego, Brady Tucker, Carlsbad 4th Ward, Carlsbad California Stake, set the record for the most tennis balls balanced in one hand with 12 tennis balls. He'd be great in a sporting goods store or the produce section at your grocery store. Just don't startle him! (Adolf Singh, 12/20/04)

MOST PEOPLE WEARING GROUCHO MARX MASKS. Who is Groucho Marx? He was one of three brothers (with Harpo and Chico) who were successful comedians and actors in the decades prior to the 1960s. One of Groucho Marx's trademarks was his bushy eyebrows, round glasses, and sizable protuberance of a nose! Silly glasses with a rubber nose have circulated at parties for the past 50 years. On December 4, 2004, a new Mormon World Record was set when 943 San Diego youth attending a multi-stake activity wore the Groucho Marx masks simultaneously. The youth represented Del Mar, Carlsbad, Escondido South, Escondido, Poway, and Penasquitos stakes. (Adolf Singh, 12/29/04)

ADOLF SINGH

Not as easy as it looks! Balancing 12 tennis balls means more than just a steady hand. It means you should have picked up that shopping cart when you first walked in.

ADOLF SINGH

Poignantly captured in this once-in-a-lifetime photo, a pensive moment is shared between Sister Groucho Marx and Sister Groucho Marx and 941 other Brother and Sister Groucho Marxes.

SHEILA KNIGHT

Malin Knight shares a smile during his marathon pogo stick jumping record. But there's more: he made 2,607 nonstop jumps during Arizona's 2007 heat wave of more than 20 straight days of temperatures in excess of 110 degrees.

MOST NONSTOP POGO STICK JUMPS. Malin Knight, age 9, of the Tolleson Ward, West Maricopa Arizona Stake, is the champion pogo stick jumper among all LDS youth with a record of 2,607 nonstop jumps in a 45-minute period, set in August 2007. "My legs are the first thing to get tired," Malin said after his record jump, explaining that everything else seems to stay "okay." For this record setting event, he needed extra witnesses, so it was off to Grandma's house and that sweltering Arizona summer heat for this fantastic achievement by a young but determined Latter-day Saint. (Author's interview with Sheila Knight [Malin's mother], 8/10/07)

FASTEST

FASTEST MORMON EVER? With space travel a good option for that "need for speed," Richard Searfoss, Bear Valley Ward, Bakersfield California East

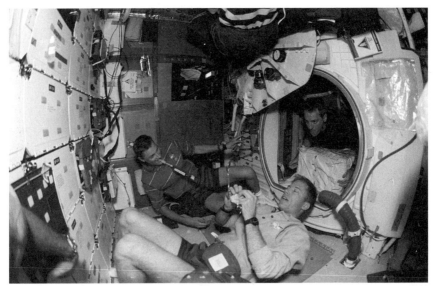

NASA

Richard Searfoss, seen here in the foreground floating on his back, is the fastest Mormon in history, with an orbital speed of 17,639 miles per hour.

Stake, may have the prize at 17,639 miles per hour (25,870 feet per second) in the space shuttle *Columbia*, April 17–May 3, 1998. He also has accumulated the longest time in space among Latter-day Saints, a total of 39 days accumulated from three flights aboard the space shuttle. He was commander of his third and last flight that took place aboard *Columbia*. When *Columbia* burned up on reentry, Brother Searfoss participated in the accident investigation. (Author's interview, 1/10/05)

FASTEST TIME TO EAT A RAW ONION (2004 WORLD RECORD). This record is nothing to cry about, but that's what happens when you eat raw onions. At a multi-stake youth activity in San Diego on December 4, 2004, Trevor Reilly, 16, Valley Center California Stake, shattered the old world record of 2 minutes 45 seconds by eating a raw onion in 1 minute 35 seconds. The onion had to weigh 7.5 ounces at the start of the contest. "The first bite choked me," he told the *San Diego North County Times*. "If I had not choked, I would have been even faster." (Adolf Singh, 12/29/04)

ADOLF SINGH

ADOLF SINGH

Do you want fries with that? Trevor Reilly meets the press while keeping a polite distance after downing a 7.5-ounce onion in world-record time.

STUART JOHNSON, *DESERET NEWS*

Ben Cook is the fastest human text messenger, beat only by a computer!

FASTEST TEXT-MESSENGER (WORLD RECORD 2006). Text messaging is using the number pad on your cell phone to spell out a text message to another person's phone. The trick is that each number has an equivalent of 3 or more letters requiring the sender to click the button multiple times to get the desired letter. In 2004, Benjamin Cook, Windsor 2nd Ward, Windsor Utah Stake, set a world record for sending the required 160-character phrase in only 57.75 seconds. Here's what competitors must type: "The razor-toothed piranhas of the genera Serrasalmus and Pygocentrus are the most ferocious freshwater fish in the world. In reality they seldom attack a human." Ben said it's like being a fast typist. "It's all thumbs, all keying with thumbs." On December 19, 2006, Ben set another world record with a blazing time of 41.52 seconds. Ben remains the fastest human and took his title with him on his mission to Tokyo, Japan, in 2007. (Author's interview, 11/18/04; www.thefreelibrary.com)

FASTEST HUMAN CONVEYOR BELT (2005 WORLD RECORD). On March 3, 2005, students at Eisenhower Junior High School in Taylorsville, Utah, set a world record for the fastest human conveyor belt. In two tries, the students conveyed an 11.4-pound mattress for 180 feet in the world-record time of 2 minutes 1 second. The old record was more than 3 minutes. (Author's interview, 3/4/05; *Deseret News*, 3/4/05)

BEST MARKSMAN. Floyd Strain was enlisted with the U.S. Marine Corps when he discovered he had a particular talent for marksmanship. He broke the range record that had stood since 1917 with a score of 332 out of a possible 340. (Floyd Strain, 1/3/05)

CLAYTON BROUGH

These students beat the old world record for a human conveyor belt by more than a full minute without sleeping on the job.

FASTEST FAST DRAW. One of the greatest all-time legends of the fast-draw handgun sport is John Phillips of the Tempe 9th Ward, Tempe Arizona Stake. He regularly placed in national and international championships, and in 1973, he won the world championship for the walking balloon timed contest (where you walk toward a balloon target awaiting a signal to fire). Brother Phillips was one of those warm and seasoned western pioneer souls who made the Church rich with devotion and quiet faith, serving a mission with his wife, Helena, when he was

GLENN KIMBER

During a tour of Israel in 1989, fast-draw champ John Phillips demonstrated his speed to fellow tour members. An Israeli archeologist, Joseph Ginat, volunteered, and Brother Phillips asked him to make a loop of his belt. The idea was that as soon as Dr. Ginat yanked that loop closed, Brother Phillips had to draw his gun and poke it through the open loop. In Brother Phillips's pants pocket was an unloaded pistol. No matter how quickly Dr. Ginat yanked the loop, it always closed on Brother Phillips's wrist, with the gun in hand and pointed at Dr. Ginat's stomach. And then Brother Phillips made things a little more difficult, as shown on the next page.

83. He passed away on January 5, 2007, at age 96, and many consider him one of the best fast draw gunsmiths that ever lived. In his two-car garage that was stuffed with a dozen metal-working machines, he was the first to use titanium to build revolver cylinders and barrels, plus a host of other related items. So, just how fast was he? Brother Phillips routinely could draw and fire in a third of a second (.32–.34 seconds was typical), and for twist-fanning style (in which the gun rests in the holster on its side instead of on its trigger), Brother Phillips could fire off a shot in the upper quarter-second range. Of that time, .145 seconds was his average to react to the "go" light, and the rest was blindingly fast hand movement. His personal best was .24 seconds. Now, who can do *anything* that fast, let alone see a signal, pull a gun with one hand, and fan the trigger with the other, like Brother Phillips could? (Gunfighter Gulch newsletter, 1/8/07; Author's interview with Helena Phillips, 6/13/07)

GLENN KIMBER

Brother Phillips had Dr. Ginat adjust the size of the loop to just ½-inch larger than the pistol's size. Brother Phillips holstered the pistol and waited. As soon as Dr. Ginat yanked on the belt, Brother Phillips had that pistol drawn and poking Dr. Ginat in the stomach with the belt tightening around his wrist. It happened so fast, fellow tour members trying to capture it on film failed to snap a photo catching the hand in motion—they could only get a before and after shot, as shown here.

TYLER KROFF

The Rubik's Cube has frustrated and dazzled millions for more than three decades. Tyler Kroff can solve any configuration in less than 14 seconds.

FASTEST SOLUTION TO A RUBIK'S CUBE. That hugely popular multi-colored, plastic cube puzzle known as a Rubik's Cube is now a world record timed event. The trick is to twist various sections until solid colors appear on each side. For most, the excruciating trial-and-error process can take hours, if not days. "I'll bet there's a better way to solve one," thought Tyler Kroff, Folsom 2nd Ward, Folsom California Stake. In his search he was introduced to the world of "speedcubing," and successfully solved his first cube in three weeks. Brother Kroff said he has since learned about 110 algorithms (fancy term for series of moves to bring the cube to a more solved "state"), but the really fast speedcubers know more than 300. Brother Kroff's best time? How about 13.60 seconds! The world record is 9.86 seconds. "I used to think the people that did this had to be geniuses,

TYLER KROFF

but if I really concentrate, I can solve a cube blindfolded in about 15 minutes . . . but that's too slow to compete. You look at the cube long enough to memorize it and put on a blindfold and solve it." How many configurations are possible? How about 43,252,003,274,489,856,000 (that's about 43 quintillion), but only one works! The minimum number of moves to solve a Rubik's Cube from any configuration is currently 26. (Author's interview, 7/20/07)

BYU NEWSNET

Brian Spotts can balance his checkbook and a dozen eggs in four minutes.

FASTEST TIME TO BALANCE A DOZEN EGGS (2005 WORLD RECORD). BYU student Brian Spotts created a new world record category on September 21, 2005, for standing a dozen raw eggs on end in the shortest time. He was in Melbourne, Australia, at the time, flown there by the Australian Egg Association for their annual convention. His record for standing a dozen eggs in 4 minutes and 2 seconds still stands. (BYU NewsNet, 9/21/05)

FASTEST MORSE CODE. Gary Hogan, Rose Park Utah Stake, was an avid radio man ever since he was in the U.S. Navy. He had his amateur radio license (K7PDN), and was known throughout Utah and elsewhere as one of the greats. He and his buddy John Luker (WB7QBC) worked together to set a world record for the fastest morse code by toe, by thumping out 35 words a minute. (*Deseret News*, 1/4/05; UARC "Microvolt," July 2005)

HOGAN FAMILY

Gary Hogan lost count of the number of students he's helped over the years master the skill of Morse code. He was so fast he even set a world record for the fastest Morse code by toe.

LONGEST

LONGEST HUMAN CONVEYOR BELT (2004 WORLD RECORD). On December 4, 2004, 1,065 youth from the seven stakes of North County, California, made the world's longest human conveyer belt when they lined up around the entire length of a high school track and passed two surfboards overhead. The boards required about 10 minutes to make the trip from start to finish. (Adolf Singh, 12/29/04)

ADOLF SINGH

Surf's up in San Diego! These youth passed two surf boards overhead to set a new world record for a human conveyor belt. The surf boards can be seen in the lower right corner of this photo.

CLAYTON BROUGH

Almost sixty feet of slide rule. Go figure . . . literally.

LONGEST SLIDE RULE (1977 WORLD RECORD). In the spring of 1977, students at Springville Junior High in Utah used assorted 8- and 12-foot-long boards, 300 nails, dozens of connecting plates, and two gallons of paint to create the world's largest working slide rule. The finished product measured 59 feet 1-1/4 inches. The old record set in 1976 measured

39 feet. And can it calculate? "It can multiply and divide a series of mathematical computations," said project co-sponsor R. Clayton Brough, Taylorsville 27th Ward, Taylorsville Utah North Central Stake. He and fellow teacher Ralph J. Snelson (mathematics instructor) were looking for a way to excite their students about math and science, and set a world record in the process. (*The Herald*, 5/1/77; *Guinness Book of World Records*, 1978 edition)

LONGEST BALLOON CHAIN (2005 WORLD RECORD). On March 3, 2005, KC Williams of West Valley, Utah, participated with one other adult and 18 middle school students to inflate more than 1,200 balloons to create a 708-foot long balloon chain in one hour. Each inflated balloon was looped and tied to make a new link in the chain. (www.graniteschools.org/jr/ eisenhower/balloon_chain.html)

LONGEST STRAW CHAIN (2005 WORLD RECORD). On December 16, 2005, students at Eisenhower Junior High School in Taylorsville, Utah, set a new world record for the longest straw chain. The old record of 3.87 miles was smashed when the 133 ninth-graders connected 42,963 standard drinking straws to produce a continuous straw chain that measured 4.57 miles in length. It took them 8 hours to complete the project.

Making the world's longest straw required teamwork and staging areas. Three-foot lengths taking 20–30 seconds each were joined into 87-foot sections, and connected at the ends with bent U-shaped flexible straws. Prior to

When these Utah students (Eisenhower Junior High) announced they were going to break a world record, their claim was, in the end, just a bunch of hot air . . . thanks to KC Williams and another volunteer who inflated the more than 1,200 balloons.

CLAYTON BROUGH

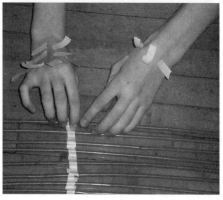

CLAYTON BROUGH

the event, students spent 15 hours puling out 120,000 individually wrapped red straws from their paper sleeves. The project was directed by R. Clayton Brough, Taylorsville 27th Ward, Taylorsville Utah North Central Stake. (Author's interview, 12/16/05)

PAUL B. SKOUSEN

Master straw makers included (circular l-r) Melissa Bateman, Haley Dawes, and Zach Hayes each of the Taylorsville 20th, North Central Utah Stake; Marcella Torrez of the Valley Park 1st Ward, Valley Park Utah Stake; Lauren Hoyt of the Taylorsville 8th Ward, Taylorsville North Utah Stake; and Jason Roper of the Taylorsville 9th Ward, Taylorsville Central Utah Stake.

CLAYTON BROUGH   CLAYTON BROUGH

LONGEST PAPER CHAIN (1977 WORLD RECORD). On April 30, 1977, 90 students from Springville Junior High School created a paper chain that measured 82,148 feet long—or more than 15 miles. This effort broke the previous record of 13.5 miles. The Springville students took only 5-1/2 hours. The event was sponsored by science teacher R. Clayton Brough, Taylorsville 27th Ward, Taylorsville Utah North Central Stake, and mathematics teacher Ralph J. Snelson. The students used 83 cubic feet of newspaper

CLAYTON BROUGH

donated by the local *Daily Herald*. Cutting the paper into strips, they stapled them to make the chain links. Brother Brough said the students used more than 225,000 staples. (Author's interview, 5/30/07; *Daily Herald*, 5/2/77)

LONGEST PAPER CLIP CHAIN (2004 WORLD RECORD). On March 26–27, 2004, some 60 ninth grade students at Eisenhower Junior High School in Taylorsville, Utah, connected 1,560,377 paper clips to make their mega-chain that measured 22.17 miles long. The previous world record was 20.44 miles set in 2001. Sixty "chain gang" students worked 24 hours with the support of dozens of other students working in three eight-hour shifts. One of the co-sponsors of the event, R. Clayton Brough, Taylorsville 27th Ward, Taylorsville Utah North Central Stake, said the event was a fantastic learning experience. "It provided many students with the opportunity to apply some of their education skills," he said, "including those related to creativity, communication, organization, logistics mathematics and economics." To keep the construction inside the school gymnasium, a large part of the floor space was set aside with 12 tall poles around which the completed chain was wrapped. Each pole had twelve 2-foot arms that could support the weight of 25 wrappings. The event was encouraged by many parents and compa-

CLAYTON BROUGH

CLAYTON BROUGH

This amazing paper clip chain was more than 22 miles long.

nies. ACCO Brands donated the 2,000,000 paper clips, a value of $7,800. Pepsi Incorporated, Gunderson Architectural Woodwork, Little Caesar's Pizza, Papa John's Pizza, Pizza Hut, and Nu Packaging also contributed. When the record was witnessed and verified, Mayor Janice Auger of Taylorsville presented the students with an official commendation and proclamation. So, with the party over, how on earth do you clean up a million and a half paper clips? "We cut it into sections and just rolled them up into giant balls of wire," Brother Brough said. "They were hoisted into a big truck and hauled off to a recycling center." (Author's interview, 5/30/07; *Deseret News*, 3/27/04; Eisenhower Junior High website)

FARTHEST TRAVELED HITCHHIKER. Neil Millman was only 17 when he made his first hitchhiking trip from California to New York, covering 3,500 miles in just 10 days. On the return trip to Utah, he traveled 4,000 miles in just four days. Not bad for a fellow with a thumb and a lot of determination. To date he's hitchhiked at least 300,000 miles, including rides aboard a Greek tanker, aircraft, freight trains, and delivering vehicles across the country. He's been robbed, beat up, in car accidents, and numerous life-threatening situations. His worldwide adventures include the Americas, Europe, Newfoundland, Canada, and Alaska. He's lived in 11 countries and traveled through 64. As part of his work to find shelter for homeless kids in Mexico, he met his wife, Margarita, and they are members of the Provo 4th Ward, Provo Utah North Park Stake. Look for his book in the future entitled "Slow Boat to China: The Adventures of a Mormon Vagabond." (Author's interview, 9/07)

NEIL MILLMAN

Neil Millman makes new friends while hitchhiking through Guatemala.

LONGEST FALL AND PARA-CHUTE JUMP (1934). (Read more in the Courage section of this book.) In the days of pioneering air flight and balloon exploration of the upper atmosphere, BYU graduate Orvil A. Anderson had just ascended to 60,613 feet in the 21-story-tall *Explorer I* high-altitude balloon when the crew's worst nightmare came to life. The bag began ripping. As the seams popped down the sides, the balloon began a rapid descent. The men were not in pressure suits and could not open the hatch of the pressurized gondola that housed them or they'd black out, as had happened on earlier balloon trials. They quickly strapped on their parachutes, and Brother Anderson's accidently ripped open.

USAF

Orvil A. Anderson and his copilots await liftoff on July 28, 1934. Shortly after this photograph was taken, the ropes were released and the balloon rose into an unexpected history.

He gathered it in his arms, and with a prayer mixed with panic, waited till the plummeting craft hit 5,000 feet to bail out. His two partners also made it out, the last bailing just 500 feet from the ground, just enough for his chute to open and slow him enough to land upright on his feet. The gondola crashed like a raw egg dropped on the floor, and the shreds of balloon followed after. Thank heavens the men lived to fly another day—which happened to come that following year when they set a world altitude record in *Explorer II*. (Can anyone help me learn if co-pilot Albert W. Stevens was LDS? Write to mormonworldrecords@gmail.com). ("My Husband the First Astronaut," by Ruth Stevens; *Improvement Era*, May 1936; *National Geographic*; various sources)

LONGEST ATV RIDE. In April 2004, four Latter-day Saints along with five close friends embarked on an amazing adventure across the United States on all-terrain vehicles (ATVs) that took them 3,247 miles in 13 days. The ATVs were modified and classified in California as automobiles and were therefore allowed on the interstate from Santa Monica, California, to New York City, New York. That didn't prevent local police along the way from pulling the group over—10 times. The purpose of the venture was to pay tribute to Elliott

Monroe, the brother of two of the riders, and to raise awareness for organ donation. Participating in the event was Greg Monroe of the Carbon Canyon Ward, Chino California Stake; Kevin Monroe of the Lakewood Third Ward, Cerritos California Stake (who also donated an organ to his deceased brother, Elliott); Brian Koontz of the Orangecrest Ward, Riverside California West Stake; and Tom Zech of the Huntington Beach Ninth Ward, North Hunting Beach California Stake. The other team members included Brian Hinsley (liver transplant recipient and first firefighter/paramedic to return to active duty after a liver transplant), Erin Erdhal (heart recipient), Matt Pendergast (tissue recipient), and Steve Strunk (diabetic). (Kevin Monroe, 1/5/05)

LONGEST TIME SWINGING. Amanda Gowans, 29th Ward, Salt Lake Riverside Stake, lives life on the upswing. On March 27, 2004 at 6 AM in a personal attempt to see how long she could swing, Amanda ended up setting a record by swinging 25 hours straight. In the process, she also managed to raise $187.59 for Shriner's Hospital. (Author's interview, 01/22/05)

GOWANS FAMILY

Amanda Gowans swings for a record-setting 25 hours straight.

LONGEST UNICYCLE RIDE, INTERRUPTED. Darrell Robison, Logan, Utah Willow Valley 1st Ward, helped raise funds for the March of Dimes on April 28, 1985, by riding his six-foot-tall unicycle 18 miles around Logan, Utah. He fell 8 or 9 times, and twice stopped for snacks, but can you fault him? That's a long drop to the pavement on each fall! He and 200 others helped raise $10,000. (Darrell Robison, 2006)

LOUDEST

LOUDEST BURP—MALE. Who in the Church can claim the loudest burp, belch, bubble, or eructation? These synonyms to the gratifying release of an air bubble in the stomach have a champion in the person of Tanner Wells of Escondido Ward, Escondido California Stake. At a multi-stake youth activity on December 4, 2004, he pumped out a burp that registered 114 decibels. In perspective,

ADOLF SINGH

A little root beer goes a loud way!

a noise above 90 decibels can damage human hearing. An amplified rock band can perform at 110 decibels while close proximity to an aircraft engine can produce 120 decibels. Good job, Brother Wells! (Adolf Singh, 12/29/04)

LOUDEST SCREAM—FEMALE. Who in the Church has the loudest scream? On December 4, 2004, Rebekah McGhee, of the Poway 2nd Ward, Poway California Stake, generated a powerful outburst scream that registered 126 decibels. In perspective, close proximity to a jet engine will result in noise above 120 decibels, and 130 decibels is the threshold of feeling pain. (Adolf Singh 12/20/04)

ADOLF SINGH

A scream louder than a jet engine? That's what the decibel meter said!

LOUDEST FINGER SNAP. Pressing the middle finger to the thumb of the same hand and sliding off quickly will produce a snapping sound known as a finger snap. The loudest recorded to date in the Church was that performed by Rachel Zachilli, of the Penasquitos Ward, Penasquitos California Stake, at a multi-stake youth activity on December 4, 2004. Her finger snap came in at 91 decibels. Putting that in perspective, this is the level at which human hearing can be put at risk of damage, while 100 decibels is the noise level of a car or truck horn. (Adolf Singh, 12/29/04)

COLLECTIONS

MOST COLLECTIONS. Who has the most collections? Mary Jane Wright, Green Mountain Ward, Lakewood Colorado Stake, reports she has 40 collections of assorted items that range from 1,000 dolls, 700 elephants, 100

rings, and 50 teapots, to dozens of others, including valentines, postcards, stamps, miniature dogs, bears, bunnies, cats, deer, pitchers, cup on saucers, sterling spoons, glass birds, china shoes, old irons, antique dishes, and the list goes on and on. (Author's interview)

MARY JANE WRIGHT

LARGEST COLLECTION OF HANDMADE MODEL AIRPLANES (2001 WORLD RECORD).

The old world record of 1,105 model airplanes held by a man in Bahrain was smashed when Robert Humphrey, West Jordan 29th Ward, West Jordan Utah East Stake, documented his collection of 1,642 in 2001. Three years later his collection had grown to 1,845.

And as long as they keep making them, Brother Humphrey will keep building them. When a kit for any particular airplane didn't exist, he just made it himself—from scratch. "My first model was an Aurora Boeing 707 I built in 1958," he said. "I was 6 years old and I still have the model in my collection. My dad bought me a bottle of black paint. But I wanted to paint it fancier so I used my mom's red fingernail polish to paint the tips of the engines."

He credits his interest in aviation to his dad, who flew P-51 Mustangs during World War II. Humphrey's favorite model is the F-4 Phantom, but there are plenty to choose from. "I have 1,711 different kits built in different schemes. They range in scale from 1/144th to 1/24th and include planes from 61 different nations." Over the past five decades, he has built more than 2,400 plastic kits. He confesses that several of his earliest models suffered the damage that comes from BB guns and firecrackers, but 45 of those were rescued and today sit in boxes at his home, awaiting repair. Starting in 1976, he began buying two of every model he could—one to build, and one to save as a backup. That

ROBERT HUMPHREY

Robert Humphrey poses with his official Guinness World Record certificate in one of several rooms of his home dedicated to housing the world's largest collection of plastic model airplanes and aircraft.

collection grows by 50–100 kits a year, and a recent count put the total of built and unbuilt at more than 7,000. He's good at it too—winning awards for contests and entering them internationally. Many of his built kits are on loan, including to the Cal-Air museum in Wyoming. While 99 percent of the kits are aircraft, he also has tanks, cars, and more than 150 science fiction models (Star Trek's Enterprise, Star Wars, etc.). He estimates the collection that fills four bedrooms in his home and several hundred feet of shelf space has cost him more than $50,000 in kits alone. (Author's interviews, 2005, 2007)

ROBERT HUMPHREY

LARGEST BINKIE COLLECTION.
During his mission to Denmark in 1969–1971, Harold D. Skousen, Brookwood Ward, Riverton Utah North Stake, began an odd collection: binkies, or more technically accurately known in the industry as pacifiers. "I started collecting them because it seemed that every time I got onto a bus or train or was walking on the street or down an aisle in a store, I would always find a binky laying there on the floor or ground. So I wondered, how many of these things can I find, and how many in each city in which I serve?" And from that point on, every mission-

HAROLD SKOUSEN

Bawling babies everywhere. Harold Skousen displays a few of the dozens of binkies he collected from the streets of Denmark.

ary in Denmark knew where to send orphaned binkies. By the end of his mission Elder Skousen had 114 binkies, each carefully labeled with the date and location of its abandonment, from which comes this amazing and new Mormon World Record that really . . . uh . . . sucks! (Author's interview, 2007)

SYLVIA ANN NEBEKER

Now I need a book! The largest bookmark collection stands at 6,347, so far!

LARGEST BOOKMARK COLLECTION. As of July 2004, the bookmark collection of Sylvia Ann Nebeker, from Washington State and a recent missionary to Salt Lake City, had grown to 6,347 separate bookmarks. It started as a hobby for one of her daughters, but Sister Nebeker took a fascination and began collecting bookmarks everywhere she and her husband traveled. Topics range from advertisements to anti-drug slogans, and from artwork to handmade. She even has 330 that advertise LDS products, slogans, scriptures, themes, and yes, advertisements! The largest category is from various bookstores (673), down to just a few dozen for holidays or depictions showing angels and promoting love. "It may not bring world peace," she said, "but it's a great collection!" (Author's interview, 3/28/04)

LARGEST COLLECTION—SPACE MEMORABILIA. For fellow space travel fans, Randy Bond of the Jordan Oaks 3rd Ward, West Jordan Utah Jordan Oaks Stake, has a collection of historic tidbits and evidences of space exploration that could become a museum if he had enough parking out front! Among his treasure of more than 3,000 items are:

• 90-plus autographs including: Neil Armstrong (first man on the moon); the *Apollo 13* survivors—Jim Lovell, Jack Swigert, Fred Haise, and Ken Mattingly; John Glenn (first American to orbit the earth); three Russian Cosmonauts; Sally Ride (first American woman in space); the three LDS astronauts, Don Lind, Jake Garn and Rick Searfoss; Alan Shepard (first American to travel into space); Judy Resnik (second American woman in space, and victim of the space shuttle *Challenger* disaster in 1986); and dozens more.

• Pieces of history: a piece of Launch Complex 26, where the first U.S. satellite was launched.

• Medallions with pieces of the *Columbia* and *Eagle* (spacecraft that landed on the moon), and pieces of the shuttle *Columbia* (first shuttle to orbit the earth in 1981, and concluding its 28th mission, it burned up on reentry over Texas in 2003).

• Out-of-production plastic scale models of the various spacecraft produced in America over the past 50 years, and more!

Among several recent acquisitions is a very rare and valuable book by Werner von Braun, a piece of the launch complex in Florida, pieces of graphite fibers that the space shuttle's solid rocket boosters are wound with, space-related stamps, and more. He also has scale models of the *Mercury, Gemini, Apollo, Vostok,* and *Soyuz* (Russian), Mir (Russian space station), *Saturn 5,* and others. (Author's interview, 1/11/06)

LARGEST PRODUCE STICKER COLLECTION. Tricia Taylor, Quail Creek Ward, Oklahoma City Oklahoma Stake, began collecting produce stickers 10 years ago. "I don't know why . . . it was just different than other collections," she said. Now with 650 stickers ranging from oranges to pul qua, she makes sure every sticker is unique. "I'm probably one of the only people to notice when apples get a new sticker style. Call it a Gala affair." Editor's note: On June 4, 2007, the UPI reported that tiny produce stickers flushed into a San Roman, California, wastewater system were floating and bypassing the screen meant to catch them at the wastewater treatment plant near San Francisco. The

TRICIA TAYLOR

Produce stickers are as varied as the nations and the fruit that carry them. Tricia Taylor's collection now exceeds 650 unique stickers.

buoyant stickers eventually worked their way into recycled water irrigation sprinklers at local parks, where they'd routinely clog the sprinkler heads. The mayors of San Ramon, Dublin, and Pleasanton, the three cities serviced by the facility, made a bet to see which city could collect the most stickers as a preventative measure. The loser would get the first turn at the water treatment plant for the chore of twice-daily cleaning the filtration screens of the pesky stickers. (Tricia Skousen Taylor, 2/6/07; UPI, 6/4/07)

LARGEST KEYCHAIN COLLECTION. Curtis Green, Valley View 7th Ward, Layton Utah Valley View Stake, never has a problem finding his keys. That is unless they become lost among the 320 keychains that make up his 30-foot 6-inch chain of memories. "The keychains are like a journal for my life. There is a story behind almost every keychain," he said. The collection was started during his mission to Oklahoma when he was given a key chain with a large *E* on it from a boy who thought his name was Elder. Since then his collection has grown with souvenirs from around the world. His favorites include a switchblade from Mexico and a key chain showing the ultrasound image of his grandchild. (Author's interview 11/16/04)

FLIERS

FIRST TO PILOT NEW FIGHTER. On December 15, 2006, Jon S. Beesley, president of the Fort Worth Texas Stake, took the controls of the brand new F-35 Lightning II stealth fighter and took it on its first test flight. After a slow pass over the air field, he pushed it to Mach 1.6 (more than 1,200 miles per hour) to the cheers and tears of those witnessing the maiden flight. Speaking to reporters afterward, Brother Beesley was jokingly heckled by one reporter who kept saying, "You just don't look like Tom Cruise," in reference to Tom Cruise's starring role in *Top Gun*. Brother Beesley shot back with a smile, "I don't pretend to be Tom Cruise. Tom Cruise pretends to be me." (*Church News*, 2/10/07)

USAF

Jon Beesley takes off at Fort Worth, Texas, to test fly the latest revision in high tech stealth technology.

FASTEST MILITARY FLIER. Gil Bertelson, now living in Utah, served 24 years in the United States Air Force flying several of the greatest planes ever designed. The hands-down fastest ever built that he flew was the reconnaissance spy plane called the SR-71, the Blackbird. This aircraft was a child of the cold war, and designed at Lockheed California's "skunk works." For nearly 30 years the SR-71 was the fastest thing in the sky, faster than any other aircraft or air-to-air missile. And were it flying today, it would still be the fastest! It set four world speed records, including one from California to Washington, DC in 64 minutes, 54 seconds, averaging more than 2,100 miles per hour (Mach 3) at altitudes exceeding 90,000 feet. At optimal speed, it covers 35 miles a minute, and to make a U-turn it needs a 175-mile radius. Meanwhile, friction with the air, even at 90,000 feet, can heat the plane's skin anywhere from 600–1500 degrees Fahrenheit. On one particular mission over the Baltic Sea and along Russia's borderlands, the air conditions made it difficult for Brother Bertelson to slow down and stay at Mach 3, and he approached Mach 3.3 (2,300 miles per hour), making him the fastest aircraft-flying Latter-day Saint ever. (John Bytheway, *Supersonic Saints* [Deseret Book, 2007],

USAF

"Talk to the tail, guys." The fastest recon aircraft ever invented could snap super-detailed spy photos and then easily outrun Soviet anti-aircraft missiles and fighters on its return to base in the U.S. Nothing could keep up with its speed of 2,100+ mph.

61)

FIRST FEMALE C-130J PILOT TO FLY INTO COMBAT.
For Janine K. Garner, joining the marines was the last
thing on her mind when she graduated from BYU. But
she gave it a try and qualified to pilot various aircraft.
When the war began in Afghanistan and Iraq, she was
deployed to the region to provide in-air refueling services using the C-130J refueling aircraft. This made her
not only the first LDS woman to fly the C-130J into a
hostile military zone, but the first female marine ever
to do that. She's based at an airfield code named Tatoonie, after the fictional home planet for the Skywalker
family featured in the early *Star Wars* movies. She and
husband, Ron, attend the Tatoonie Branch. With a reputation for knitting
during auto-pilot flying time, Sister Garner's commanding officer joked by
announcing, "The knitting lamp is now lit," meaning, she could pull out the
yarn and go to work. As a thank you, she knitted a very pretty pink cover for

JANINE K. GARNER

Janine K. Garner

JANINE K. GARNER

Before (the official USAF cover)

JANINE K. GARNER

After (with a little feminine touch)

Sister Garner's handiwork appears in the cockpit of her C-130J.

JANINE K. GARNER

her commander's $500,000 Heads Up Display (HUD), shown below. Pink looks so good on a marine. (Author's email interview, 4/4/06)

RAY JOHNSON

Ray Johnson in a pose he's made hundreds of times over the years, this time holding two record-breaking trout he just caught—all in a day's work.

OTHER AMAZING ACHIEVEMENTS

BEST FISHERMAN IN THE HISTORY OF THE WORLD—2006. The lofty and ominous claim of "best in the world" bestowed by prominent sports fishing experts and declared in more than 400 sports and fishing publications around the world is most certainly well deserved for Ray Johnson, Manila Utah Ward, Green River Wyoming Stake.

Brother Johnson is a Utah native with hundreds of world and state fishing record certificates piled up all over his house. And not just Ray, but his wife, children, and the family as a whole are world record holders as well.

• **Most Fish Catches, Family (2008 World Record).** As of this printing (2008), the Ray Johnson family has set more than 200 official world records and dozens of state records.

• **Most Fly-rod Fish Catches, Family (2008 World Record).**

• **Most Record-sized Fish Caught, Females, any age—2008.** Lisa Johnson, 13, is listed as catching more world- and state-record fish than any other female on record.

• **Most Record-sized Fish Caught, Males, under 18—2008.** Kirk Johnson, 15, is listed as catching more world- and state-record fish than any other underage male on record.

• **First Mormon Inducted into the Fishing Hall of Fame.** In 1984, Ray Johnson became the first Latter-day Saint as well as native Utahn to be inducted to the National and World Fishing Hall of Fame.

Keeping track of the Johnson family fishing records is a nearly impossible task. Since Brother Johnson first introduced himself to the keeper of the Mormon world records in 2004, his family has racked up dozens of additional records over the intervening years. And because records can be beat, many of theirs have fallen to another skilled fisherman somewhere in the world, but that doesn't stop their amazing level of achievements from growing year after year.

Fishing records can be established for any particular species of fish according to a fish's weight and length, and the equipment used— line poundage, reel or no reel, fly, all tackle, etc. Johnson and his family, for example, have set 63 records for kokanee salmon since 1985 using dozens of different line weights from 2- to 20-pound test line.

RAY JOHNSON

Lisa Johnson, age 7, holds this massive world record lake trout caught by her dad, Ray, on July 9, 1998. It weighed in at 52 pounds 1 ounce and was 46-1/2 inches long.

The longest fish Ray caught was a tiger muskie that measured 53-1/2 inches, the longest ever caught in Utah. His heaviest fish was a lake trout that weighed 52 pounds 1 ounce, the heaviest ever caught in Utah as of 2006. His son Kirk caught the second heaviest in Utah at 51 pounds 14 ounces, and his daughter caught the third heaviest at 51 pounds 12 ounces.

The National and World Fishing Hall of Fame credits him with 2 all tackle records, 48 line class records for trolling and casting tackle, 16 line class records on fly-casting, 4 records in pole/line/no reel division, and 7 Utah state records. His accumulation of astonishing achievements includes record catches of 11 different species, registered records in 7 different waters, and 16 different line poundages for his records in 24 different categories. He has fished on almost every continent, including Russia several times, and keeps pulling in the giants of just about every sport fishing species he can find. A dozen of his records will never be beaten now because some of those species he caught years ago are on endangered lists today.

At age 11, Johnson invented a lure that he has since refined and used thousands of times over the years to set his many records.

RAY JOHNSON

Jolene, Kirk (age 7), and Lisa (age 6) hold a giant lake trout caught at Flaming Gorge by Kirk in 1997. It weighed in at 51-3/4 pounds, a new world record.

"The Legend Lure," invented by Ray Johnson as an 11-year-old fishing enthusiast in Salt Lake City. His lure succeeded where others failed—it overcame the obstacle of making a lure look like a fish and still wiggle when dragged through the water.

Sales of his patented "Legend Lure" exceed 600,000 and can be found dangling or dragging through waters around the world. It draws fish like nothing else in the world. "Fish see it, swim towards it, open their mouth and clamp on," Johnson says. And typically he can haul in 30 to 50 pound fish that experts say should average only around five pounds.

Some sample quotes about Brother Johnson's amazing achievements from national sources:

People Magazine (1981): "Ray Johnson is indisputably the best angler in the world—the world's greatest fisherman!"

Fishing Hall of Fame (1985): "The 'legend of Ray Johnson' prevails."

Sports Afield (1976): "He has caught more larger brown, rainbow, cutthroat, and lake trout from public water than any other angler in history."

Rocky Mountain Sportsman (1986): "He is the most famous trophy trout fisherman."

Fishing and Boating Illustrated (1988): "Ray Johnson is a fisherman's fisherman."

Argosy (1978): "No angler in modern history . . . has caught as many brown trout over 10 or 20 pounds as has Johnson."

The In-Fisherman (1989): "Ray Johnson is the 'king' of world fishing records and the world's best fisherman! He has caught more record-size fish of different species and more big trout from public waters than anyone living and than anybody in history!"

Action Fishing (1982): "Year in and year out, Johnson is by far the most successful trophy trout fisherman."

Western Outdoors (1983): "Ray Johnson catches fish like no man before him. He is the world's greatest fisherman. He is a living legend. He is a hero, a mod-

U.S. FISHING HALL OF FAME

The Fishing Hall of Fame in Kansas City, Missouri. The Johnsons were inducted to it in 1984.

46

ern-day legend."

Fishing Hall of Fame (1985): "There is no question that Ray Johnson is a living legend."

PONY EXPRESS RIDERS. Who among the Saints participated in the short-lived but legendary Pony Express? One rider was Amos R. Wright, pictured here at about the time he rode. Brother Wright went on to serve several missions to the Sho- shone Indians of Wyoming's Wind River Reservation. Read

Amos R. Wright, at about the time he rode for the Pony Express.   GLORIA WRIGHT

more about that amazing conversion story in his brief biography (see the index for Wright, Amos R.). (Gloria Wright, 3/23/05)

PONY EXPRESS—FASTEST. The most famous of all Pony Express riders was Robert "Pony Bob" Haslam. He was born in 1840 in London, England, when his family joined the Church, and moved to Utah. The Pony Express was organized in 1860 to move the mail from St. Joseph, Missouri, to lands westward. St. Joseph was as far west as the railroad was built. Brother Haslam's routes were typically 75 miles, but he made history when he covered 380 miles in 40 hours on a round trip from Friday's Station at Lake Tahoe to Smith's Station in central Nevada and back again. He set another

PAUL B. SKOUSEN

World's largest get well card.

record carrying news of Abraham Lincoln's election by taking a 120 mile ride in 8 hours and 10 minutes. The Pony Express was disbanded in 1861.

LARGEST GET WELL CARD. After the 2004-05 devastating floods in St. George that destroyed homes and lives, a get well card campaign was started that netted best wishes from thousands, many from around the world. Pictured here, Dave Watson, chairman of the fund-raising efforts for flood relief; Georgia Carpenter, formerly of Cedar Fort, Inc.; and Paul Skousen, that writer guy. (Author 3/6/05)

BEN AND BRITTANY SKOUSEN

The Church's emphasis on family and its eternal nature attracts converts from all walks of life. It helps members build the best and most secure nurturing environment for raising Saints old and young—such as Jessica Skousen, above. And from such work comes a unique and positive force for good in the earth —the LDS human being.

THE LDS HUMAN BEING

MORMON ACHIEVEMENTS BY THE NUMBERS

9—Consecutive father/son descendants named Richard Hemsley

13—Sets of twins in one ward

308—Days between two full-term births

73,000—Man hours donated by Latter-day Saints for Hurricane Katrina victims.

AGE

OLDEST LIVING MEMBER. As of this writing (August 2007), the oldest living member of the Church, and possibly the oldest living person in the world, is Sister Amelia Costa dos Santos, Ajuricaba Ward, Manaus Brazil Ponta Negra Stake, who turned 119 on May 15, 2007 (she was born May 15, 1888). She was baptized at age 111 by her grandson Nilzomar Souza. Elder Kip Lambert of South Jordan, Utah, met Sister dos Santos while serving his mission and joked with her, saying, "Boy, you're old. There must have been a lot of sins washed away when you were baptized." To which she replied, "Elder, I never felt cleaner." She has 15 children, 96 grandchildren, and more than 100 great-grandchildren. (*Church News*, 8/18/07)

DOS SANTOS FAMILY

At a 119 years old, Sister dos Santos was unofficially the oldest living person in the world in 2007.

OLDEST MAN. Who is the oldest living man in the Church to see the turn of two millenniums? As of 2006, it was Brother Torkil Dresso, Frederiksberg Ward, Copenhagen Denmark Stake, who turned 107 on March 27, 2006. A month prior to his birthday, he walked unaided to the pulpit in his ward to bear his

KAREN PEDERSON

Torkil Dresso, 107 in 2006

testimony. And to what did Brother Dresso attribute his longevity? "I don't drink, I don't smoke, and that would have something to do with it," he said, "because there is no one in my family who ever came up to this age." He was born March 27, 1898, was baptized in 1953, and passed away in October 2006. (Niels and Karen Pederson, 3/28/06)

SIZE

SHORTEST WOMAN. Melodie Winn is the shortest LDS women on record at 3 feet 3 inches, and 28 years old. She's a teacher in her Country Crossing Sixth Ward, Country Crossing Utah Stake, and was one of those great inspirational individuals nominated to carry the torch for the 2002 Winter Olympics in Salt Lake City. She enjoys performing on stage, and after her graduation from BYU, she performed in New York, Chicago, and other venues. "I am a Little Person that was born into a family where everyone else is average sized," she said. "It is genetic but I don't know much about it." She stays busy, including serving a family history mission for 12 months. (Melodie Winn, 7/4/05)

MELODIE WINN

Melodie Winn displays the Olympic torch she carried in 2002.

TWINS, BABIES, FAMILIES

LOWE FAMILY

Not quite twins, but the next best thing—Kyrie and Brayden are about 10 months and 4 days apart.

SHORTEST INTERVAL BETWEEN FULL-TERM BIRTHS. Ten months, 3 days, 23 hours, 38 minutes is the shortest interval between full-term births, by Eric and Tara Lowe. Their daughter Kyrie Alyssa Lowe was born on July 1, 2003, at 8:32 AM, and their son Brayden Tyler Lowe was added to the family on May 5, 2004 at 8:10 AM. That's an interval of 308 days, 23 hours and 38 minutes, or 444,938 minutes. (Eric Lowe, 9/27/05)

Rosalie Despain Urland and her husband report they had two sons born in the same year. The first was born March 1, 1978, and the second was born December 25, 1978—a span of 9 months, 24 days. Missing from this inspiring family-building feat is whether or not the second child went full term, which is a challenging part of this record's requirements. Sister Urland, wherever you are, please write me at mormonworldrecords@gmail.com! (Rosalie Despain, 12/2/04)

WHAT ARE THE ODDS? Eileen Clasby reports a highly unlikely convergence of dates with the birth of her two sons on the same day, exactly eight years apart. But not just any day. It was leap day, that added day in February that comes along every four years. Justin was born on February 29, 1988, and Hayden was born on February 29, 1996. And for those doubters out there, both boys were born on their doctor-prescribed due dates! (Eileen Clasby, 11/11/04)

EILEEN CLASBY

Justin and Hayden Clasby beat the most amazing odds of the year, on leap day.

MOST CONSECUTIVE TWINS. History was made on May 19, 2002. That's the day that twins Nathan Benjamin and Alexander William Bartholoma were born, marking the fourth consecutive generation of the Taylor family to produce twins. It all began in 1919 when Jedidiah and Margaret Ritchie Taylor anxiously awaited the birth of their new babies. And the rest is history!

October 29, 1919—Gail and Dale Ritchie Taylor, Idaho (parents: Jedidiah and Margaret Ritchie Taylor)

February 5, 1955—Janet and Joyce Taylor, Idaho (parents: Gail and Jean Evelyn Carpenter Taylor)

September 4, 1981—Debra Jean and Daniel Dean Haroldsen, Idaho (parents: Brian and Janet Taylor Haroldsen)

JANET HAROLDSEN

Twins (top, l-r): Dale Taylor, Janet and Joyce Taylor, Debra and Daniel Haroldson with twins Nathan and Alex Bartholoma seated between them.

May 19, 2002—Nathan Benjamin and Alexander William Bartholoma (parents: Christopher Michael and Debra Jean Haroldsen Bartholoma). (Janet Haroldsen, 7/16/07)

NARDA EMETT

MOST TWINS IN ONE WARD. Seeing double is something that happens a lot in the Overlake 1st Ward, Tooele Utah North Stake. That's because as of March 2006, it had 13 sets of twins, all 18 or under.

- Sierra Demetria and Savannah Rachelle Emett, November 16, 2004
- Annie Marx and Jack Christopher Olsen, February 26, 2001
- Sierra Mackenzie and Jordan Thomas Brooks, March 23, 1994
- Brenden Cole and Braylie Nichole Jones, July 26, 1998
- Gillian Dianne and Julia Danielle Lund, January 8, 1993
- Forrest Dowling and Prescott Thomas Ward, November 9, 1992
- Anna Elizabeth and Brendan Campbell Ward, August 1, 1997
- Frankie Marie and April Lynn Ostrander, April 3, 1988
- Daniel Jaime and David Carlos Lords, June 19, 1990
- Alicia Mariah and Felicia Alejandra Lords, December 22, 2001
- Kyrstanne Kaye and Keano Wade Idom, July 15, 1999
- K. and C. Lauren, August 1, 1997
- D. and B. Ryan, November 12, 2001

(Source: Overlake 1st Ward, Tooele Utah North State)

QUINTUPLETS

AMERICAN WEIGHT RECORD (2007)—THE WILKINSON FAMILY, ARIZONA. After two children, Jayson and Rachelle Wilkinson, Austin Texas Stake, had difficulty having a third child. They visited a fertility expert who told them there was a 20 percent chance of twins, a 5 percent chance of triplets. After the pregnancy took hold, an MRI told the amazing truth—five babies! The doctor told the Wilkinsons to reduce that to twins and painted a gloomy picture of physical or mental disorders. That possibility brought a very dark feeling with it, and the family knew they should move forward with welcoming all five into their home. A Phoenix doctor experienced with multiple births took over and directed Sister Wilkinson through the risky pregnancy. She was put on a 5,000 calorie per day diet and was ordered into bed rest for the last 13 weeks. At a petite 5 foot 2 inches, she was still able to carry the babies for 34 weeks. This beat the national average by 5 weeks. The babies arrived healthy and happy with a combined weight of 21 pounds, 7.2 ounces—more than 6 ounces over the prior record. The babies were Kassidy, Kaydence, Kyndall, Rustin, and Ryder. (*Church News*, 9/1/07; www.wilkinsonquints.org)

WILKINSON FAMILY

The Wilkinson family with their brand new quintuplets in 2007.

THE HORTON FAMILY, ILLINOIS. The Hortons had been trying for a third child using fertility drugs when Sister Taunacy Horton announced she was pregnant—and not with just their third child, but five new little ones. Meanwhile, Brother Horton had been serving in Iraq, taking a team of Marines he had trained into their very first combat experience. Five days before the birth of his quintuplets, Horton was wounded in a grenade attack south of Baghdad. He was heavily sedated and on the verge of losing a foot to amputation when word came of the births. He survived the ordeal, kept his foot, and was able to rejoice with his wife as she related the exciting news to him over phone on October 12, 2004. The children all weighed in at under 2 pounds, and survived. The Hortons were members of the Oswego, Chicago Illinois Ward. (*Deseret News*, 10/13/04)

MOST BABY DELIVERIES BY C-SECTION. From 1970 to 1982, Dana Thelin, Provo Utah South Stake, delivered by c-section all 8 of her children. As a volunteer in the Provo School District, she was chosen as the 1990 National Volunteer of the Year, and received her award at the White House from Barbara Bush. The First Lady asked, "How do you do so much for your local community while raising those eight children?" Sister Thelin just smiled. (Dana Thelin, 12/20/04)

MOST ADOPTED CHILDREN. It was 1993 when a premature baby boy, only 2.3 pounds, was found nearly dead from exposure in a sewage channel in near freezing temperatures near Colombo, Brazil. He had been there in the rain with no clothing for most of the night. The paramedic who rescued him and cared for him during his 45-day stay in a pediatric intensive care unit was Ozair Jesus Ribeiro Filho, a recent convert to the LDS Church. The little boy had no home or parents, so after he regained his strength, Brother Ribeiro and his wife, Rosicler, adopted him, bringing their family size to four. Over the years they adopted others until by 2007 their family had grown to 23—Brother and Sister Ribeiro, their three biological children, and 18 adopted children. They live in the Cuaraituba Ward, Curitiba Boa Vista Brazil Stake. Brother Ribeiro has been a bishop and counselor in the stake presidency, and Sister Ribeiro is the seminary teacher. Because of their example, 13 other families have adopted 20 orphans. Such events have helped the Riberio family spread the gospel to neighbors and friends everywhere. (*Church News,* 6/16/07; email interview with Ana Claudia Soli)

MOST CHILDREN. Ray and Brenda Lewis, Eagle, Idaho, began their family on the heels of tragedy. Brother Lewis's first wife and full-term son, David, were killed in a car accident in 1974, leaving him with two living daughters. He later married Brenda, and together they had 13 more children in a span of 25 years—a total of 16 children. Brother and Sister Lewis never owned a van and had to take two cars to Church, and to eat they needed two dinner tables with benches at home! (Shiree [Lewis] Christensen, 1/30/06)

MOST CHILDREN. Vean and Tonya Woodbrey, Aspen Meadows Third Ward, Spanish Fork Utah East Stake, have 16 children, all single births, and equally divided with eight boys, eight girls. (Kelly Woodbrey, 12/2/04)

CORINNE JENSEN

Layton and Betty Ott

QUICKEST MARRIAGE AFTER A MISSION. Elder Layton Ott was serving in the Southern States Mission during 1950–1952 when he met Betty Byrd in Arkansas. He and his companion taught her the gospel, and she was baptized three months into his mission. Elder Ott and Betty were attracted but kept the rules. Elder Ott's mission president recognized a potential marriage there and encouraged Elder Ott to propose while he had the chance but to finish his mission before anything else. With his companion as witness, he proposed on bended knee, and Betty headed to Utah to make plans. After Elder Ott was released, he arrived in Utah on June 28, 1952, a Saturday night, at precisely 10 PM. The following Monday, June 30, 1952, only 36 hours after he arrived home, they were married in the Logan Temple. They celebrated their 52nd anniversary before Brother Ott passed away in 2004. They had seven children, numerous grandchildren, and a happy ending to a wonderful love story. Sister Ott resides in the Green Valley 4th Ward, Green Valley Utah Stake (St. George, Utah). (Corinne Jensen, 11/29/04)

MOST HUSBANDS IN A LIFETIME. This good sister has passed away, and for now, she will only be known as D.P. But D.P. had, for whatever reason, been married and divorced a record 15 times. Is this the new Mormon World Record? Any challengers? (Interview with D.P.'s attorney, Lew Hansen, 12/06/04)

FIRST ONLINE LOVERS TO MARRY. Thanks to the emerging technologies and opportunities linked to the Internet, singles all over the world have found true love online, with many deciding to marry—even in the temple. The question is, who can claim the record for being the first LDS to be married from an online relationship? In September 1997, Catherine Armstrong (online name "Cotton Candy") says she and her new online best friend, Barry Inscore ("Bearman"), fell in love thanks to some dandy keyboarding between the two of them. With both of them emerging from divorces and with 13 kids (her, 7; him, 6), neither of them were very encouraged that life might bring true love again. But they found themselves chatting with others of their age group in a side room for those over 50. Barry said Catherine's sense of humor was so much like his, they clicked over to "the barn" to carry on. And from there, things just blossomed. After many weeks of exchanges and getting to know each other's inner souls,

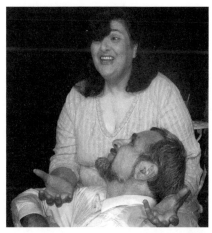

CATHERINE INSCORE

"Cotton Candy" and "Bearman" may be the first LDS couple to discover each other on the Internet, fall in love, and propose to get married, sight unseen!

Barry decided it was time to make the plunge. They still had not seen photos of each other, but they knew one another's hearts.

The night he logged on to propose marriage, Barry discovered to his horror that an impersonator had been sending false messages to Catherine and had abruptly dissolved the relationship. Barry was frantic and prayed that Catherine would log back on so he could clean up the mess and make his formal proposal. She bravely did log on, and Barry was able to salvage what might have been a mean and terrible tragedy.

When he proposed marriage, Catherine said the message made her break down in tears of joy because someone wanted her sight unseen. It was a love built on a foundation many couples never find until years later.

Barry played a trick on her. She knew he was LDS, and she was a devout but non-practicing Catholic. He told her he'd have a missionary deliver a Book of Mormon so she'd understand his faith a little better, and then he would arrive the following day. So, Barry dressed in a white shirt, put on a missionary name tag, and delivered the book himself. He found her in the worst possible way. She'd been cleaning all day, wearing a badly faded stained house dress, barefoot, and just not in a mood to talk to some pesky missionary. But Barry continued the prank and read aloud the testimony written inside the Book of Mormon, and then broke into a Beatles song, giving away his true identity. It was a melting embrace and the start of a delightful companionship that was later sealed in the temple. Today, Cotton Candy and Bearman live in the El Paseo Ward, Yucca Valley California Stake. (Barry and Catherine Inscore, 6/16/07)

MOST SIBLINGS TO SEE GOLDEN WEDDING ANNIVERSARY. The Forsyth family (Neil Snow and Chloe Rosealtha Hatch) have a great longevity record that could be tough to beat. All seven children and their spouses lived and stayed married long enough to see their 50th wedding anniversaries, following the pattern set by their parents who celebrated their 50th in 1961.

(Parents) Neil and Chloe (Hatch) Forsyth, married 12/20/11, had their 50th in 1961.

Neil and Gladys (Butler) Forsyth had their 50th on 12/14/89.

George and June (Hinman) Forsyth had their 50th on 5/14/93.

Mylo and Matilda (Meier) Forsyth had their 50th on 4/12/96.

FORSYTH FAMILY

Duane and Verna (Neilson) Forsyth had their 50th on 4/3/95.
Ruth (Forsyth) and Robert Horne had their 50th on 12/27/95.
Garth and Jean (Campbell) Forsyth had their 50th on 10/14/98.
Bryce and June (Volk) Forsyth had their 50th on 2/23/05.

(Source: Forsyth family members, 2006)

MILITARY

FIRST LDS CHAPLAIN. John William Boud was the first Navy and LDS chaplain in history, and received his appointment of "Chaplain with the Rank of Lieutenant" in the United States Navy on July 31, 1941. The assignment had been approved by President Heber J. Grant. His law firm with Bruce McConkie, Milton Hess, and Larry Summerhays had to be broken up so Brother Boud could enter the service at the outbreak of World War II. He served four years in San Diego and the Hawaiian Islands, organizing LDS meeting groups. In the early part of his assignment, he oversaw the funeral services and burying of LDS sailors lost in the attack on Pearl Harbor. (Thomas J. Boud, 1/12/05)

MEDAL OF HONOR WINNERS. Submissions requested! Do you know of any Latter-day Saints who won the U.S. Medal of Honor, or its equivalent in other countries? If so, please let us know. Those in the U.S. are:

• Mervin S. Benion, son-in-law of J. Reuben Clark. Awarded for keeping the USS *West Virginia* engaged in battle and floating upright despite fatal wounds.

• Bernie Fisher, for landing his one-seat aircraft on an airstrip overrun by the enemy in Vietnam to rescue a downed pilot. (George H. Hill III, 5/13/05)

SCOUTING

MOST EAGLE SCOUTS IN ONE FAMILY. With only 2 percent of boys entering the scouting program ever earning their Eagle, 9, 10, 11, or more Eagles in one family is probably a world record for the Boy Scouts of America, not to mention a new Mormon World Record. Here are the record holders to date:

11—In 2005, Brother and Sister Lynn T. Dayton of the Lakeview 6th Ward, Orem Lakeview Stake, reported that all 11 of their sons earned their

Eagles: Lynn Taylor Jr., Kenneth, Christopher, Brendon, David, Jared, Adam, McKay, John, Joseph, and Perry. (Lynn T. Dayton, 1/1/05)

THOMAS FAMILY

The Thomas family Eagles Nest

11—In 2001, the Larry and Sherry Thomas family of the North Las Vegas Nevada Stake had all eleven of their boys earn their Eagle Scout Award, leaving their lone sister, Elaine, a very proud eaglet in this nest! The Eagles are Darrin, Charles, Robby, Gordon, Devin, Eddie, Ralph, Gilbert, Rex, DeCall, and Harvey. (DeCall Thomas, 11/10/04)

11—In 2006, the John W. and Sharon R. Boud family had eleven Eagle Scouts, including the father. In addition, two foster sons and an Indian placement student each earned their Eagle Scout awards while living with the family, bringing the total to 14. (Thomas J. Boud, 1/12/05)

10—In 2006, the Fred and Joyce Dupaix family of the Union Ward in Sandy, Utah, had 10 Eagle Scouts in their family: Fred (dad), Tom, Harold, Steve, Brian, Geogrey, Dan, Richard, Mike and Joseph. (Garth Limburg, 3/28/06)

PORTER FAMILY

10—In 2005, the Porter family of the Vineyard 1st Ward, Sunset Heights Stake, had 10 Eagle Scouts, and 10 of the 12 served missions. (Tim Porter, 2/20/05)

The Porter family

FIRST INDIAN TO EARN EAGLE SCOUT AWARD. This category is a tricky one because the word *Indian* is too general, and numerous tribes are not well represented. Also, this record is a tough one to uncover, so contributions are invited and welcome. For all future editions, we'll break down "First Indian" to their specific tribe.

FILE PHOTO

Lee Tashnebully

FIRST NAVAJO TO EARN EAGLE SCOUT AWARD. In 1927, Lee Tashnebully became the first Navajo to earn his Eagle Scout Award. He also earned 22 merit badges beyond the required number. He was a star center for his high school football team and later became one of the famous "Code Talkers" during World War II. He and his wife, Nancy, joined the Church in 1953. Sister Tashnebully's father

helped negotiate with the other Navajo clans for permission for the missionaries to preach on the Navajo reservation. ("Treks to the San Juan Basin" July
1992; Charles C. Wheeler Jr., 8/7/05)

MOST MERIT BADGES. In 2007, Chris Haskell, 17, of Troop 918, Elk
Ridge 2nd Ward, Payson Utah Stake, officially earned the last of 120
available merit badges toward earning his 19th Eagle Palm, one of the
highest honors in the Boy Scouts of America program. Which of the 120
was the toughest? "I was a shy kid at the time," Chris said. "Communications was the hardest. You have to speak before a couple of groups. I had
a hard time with that and Public Speaking merit badge." His work on the
Chemistry merit badge sparked an interested in the sciences, and Chris
has decided to look at the sciences for a college major after his mission.
(Author's interview, 9/6/07)

ODDS AND ENDS

MOST TO WIN A TRIP TO THE NATIONAL 4-H CONGRESS. 4-H is a great
idea sponsored by the USDA with the goal of "engaging youth to reach their
fullest potential." The name is derived from the four *H*s: Head, Heart, Hands,
and Health. Youth from ages 5 to 21 in all 50 states participate. There are
some 100,000 clubs with 9 million members who learn leadership and life
skills. Their motto is "To make the best better," and their slogan is "Learn by
doing." In the early days, 4-H focused on agricultural knowledge, but today
its emphasis is also on computer science, geographic information systems,
and public speaking. Each year select members are sent to a 4-H Congress
in Atlanta, Georgia. The Vean Robert Woodbrey and Tonya Woodbrey family had 16 children, 15 of whom won a trip to the National 4-H Congress.
(Kelly Woodbrey, 12/2/04)

**LAST SURVIVING GRANDDAUGHTER OF
BRIGHAM YOUNG.** Sister Marian Young Morgan, the last living granddaughter of Brigham
Young, passed away November 22, 2004, at the age
of 105. She was the daughter of Brigham Young Jr.,
a member of the Quorum of the Twelve and counselor to his father, President Brigham Young. She was
born January 15, 1899, in Fruitland, New Mexico.
(*Church News*, 12/4/04)

FILE PHOTO
Marian Young Morgan

LONGEST STRING OF SAME NAMES. Richard Hemsley, Spencer Ward, Kaysville Utah Stake, reports he's in a family with a wonderful string of sons named Richard. All but the first were baptized into the Church. The first Richard has long since had his work done for him.

1. Richard Hemsley (born 1775)
2. Richard Hemsley (born 1801, baptized 1855)
3. Richard Hemsley (born 1836, baptized 1855)
4. Richard Hemsley (born 1864, baptized 1872)
5. Richard Hemsley (born 1889, baptized 1897)
6. Richard Hemsley (born 1912, baptized 1920)
7. Richard Hemsley (born in Idaho Falls, baptized)
8. Richard Hemsley (born in Willard, Utah, baptized)
9. Richard Hemsley (born in Kaysville, Utah, and will be baptized)

(Source: Richard "Bryan" Hemsley, 12/7/04)

FAMOUS INDIAN GUIDE. Though not LDS, John Baptiste Charbonneau was a famous Indian guide who helped travelers moving between Sante Fe and San Diego. The significance of Charbonneau can be found on the golden U.S. dollar coin minted in 2000. Look for the image of Sacagawea and notice the little child she is carrying on her back while helping the Lewis and Clark expedition. That's John Baptiste Charbonneau, born February 11, 1805, and later the guide for the Mormons, who went trekking to California in 1847. (Thanks to Curtis R. Allen for this tidbit, 12/06/04)

SERVICE

MOST SERVICE-MINDED. In 2005, Hurricane Katrina wiped out an area the size of Kansas when it flooded New Orleans and environs, doing some $100 billion in damage with 145-mph wind blasts. Five Latter-day Saints were among the 700 who died. The storm pulverized 90 percent of the buildings on a 130-mile stretch of coast. Within two weeks the Church had dispatched 140 truckloads of supplies and commodities, equaling 5.6 million pounds, or 2,800 tons. Thousands of Mormon Helping Hands donated 73,000 man-hours to help members and nonmembers alike—as many as they could. At one point, more than 4,000 Katrina victims were housed in 20 LDS church buildings. (LDS.org; *Church News*, 9/17/05)

LAST-MINUTE ADDITION!

OLDEST IDENTICAL TWINS. Engla Hess Thomsen (Christensen) and Thora Hess Thomsen (Petersen), both of Salt Lake City, celebrated their 95th birthday on October 15, 2007, making them the oldest identical twins in the Church, and possibly in the U.S. They were born into the Church in Silkeborg, Denmark, in 1912, and moved to the U.S. shortly after World War II. They have both been active members of the LDS Church all their lives. (Neva Thompson, 11/25/07)

NEVA THOMPSON

Engla and Thora, going strong at 95 and counting!

NEVA THOMPSON

Engla and Thora Thomsen at age 21, strolling through the Danish country-side.

NEVA THOMPSON

Engla and Thora Thomsen at age 5, in 1917.

61

OSMOND FAMILY

George (10/13/17–11/6/07) and Olive Osmond (5/4/25–5/9/04), parents of the famed Osmond singers, brought new meaning to the word *fame*. Their dignity, foresight, hard work, and passion for living a balanced family life within the gospel of Jesus Christ launched their children on a path of amazing fame and success. With family values at the central core of all things, Brother and Sister Osmond instilled in their nine children a passionate work and gospel ethic. This strong beginning and foundation carried these young entertainers safely through the vicissitudes and temptations of life while in the lofty but risky lime-light of worldwide fame.

FAME

MORMON ACHIEVEMENTS BY THE NUMBERS

1—Number of Latter-day Saints on Japan's National Congress
475—Days a Mormon reigned as Miss World
2,520,700—Dollars won by Ken Jennings on JEOPARDY!

POLITICS

JAPAN. In 2004, Sister Keiko Itokazu became the first member of the Church to hold national office in Japan. She won a seat in July to the House of Councilors in Japan's National Diet (Congress) by a huge landslide. It was such a commanding victory that the local media announced her victory just five minutes after the polls had closed, based on exit polling. Before that election, Sister Itokazu had served 12 years in the Okinawa Prefecture Assembly. (*Church News,* 12/25/04; photo by Japan Times)

FILE PHOTO
Keiko Itokazu

MOST POLITICALLY ACTIVE LDS FAMILY. Who among the generations of Latter-day Saints has the most political involvement on any elected level? Dave and Laurel Udall sent in an amazing collection of family members who have participated in a dozen major political offices.

FILE PHOTO
Sen. Morris Udall, AZ

David King Udall—Arizona state senate (and first Arizona Temple president)

John H. Udall—Mayor of Phoenix

Nicholas Udall—Mayor of Phoenix and Arizona Judge of the Superior Court

Jesse Udall—Supreme Court judge for Arizona

Morris Udall—U.S. Congressman (Arizona) and ran for U.S. President in 1975.

FILE PHOTO
Sen. Gordon Smith, OR

FILE PHOTO

Rep. Stewart Udall, AZ

Sam Udall—Gilbert, Arizona, Board of Education

Earl Udall—City manager (Provo, Utah; Merced, California)

Gordon Smith—U.S. Senate (R-Oregon); his mother was a Udall

Mark Udall—U.S. Congressman (Colorado)

Tom Udall—Attorney General, New Mexico, and U.S. Congressman

Levi Udall—Arizona Supreme Court Justice

Stewart Udall—U.S. Congressman (Arizona) and Secretary of Interior for President John F. Kennedy and Lyndon B. Johnson.

(Source: Dave and Laurel Udall, Lindon, Utah)

FIRST LDS CONGRESSMAN. An early member of the Church from New York City, John H. Bernhisel, MD, lived in the Mansion House with the Smith family and later spent the night in Carthage Jail. On the way there, it was Dr. Bernhisel to whom Joseph Smith privately told, "I go like a lamb to the slaughter . . ." During the migration west, Brigham Young sent Dr. Bernhisel and five others back to dedicate the Nauvoo Temple. In Salt Lake City, Dr. Bernhisel was elected as Utah's first congressman and served in the 32nd Congress, and in the three succeeding Congresses (March 4, 1851–March 3, 1859); he did not seek office in 1858 and resumed his practice of medicine in Salt Lake City but was again elected to the 37th Congress (March 4, 1861–March 3, 1863). Dr. Bernhisel served a total of four terms in Congress, meeting personally with Presidents Lincoln, Fillmore, and Pierce, and Daniel Webster, presenting each of them with a Book of Mormon. (Randy Bell, Rancho Santa Margarita Ward, California, 4/18/06)

PAGEANTS

Miss World

1951—Kerstin (Kiki) Håkansson, who was also Miss Sweden, was the winner of the very first Miss World beauty pageant in 1951 and later joined the Church. Kiki also holds the record for the longest reign as Miss World—475 days. (Randy Bell, Rancho Santa Margarita Ward, California, 4/18/06)

FILE PHOTO

Kerstin Håkansson

FILE PHOTO
Laurie Richardson

National Mother of the Year
2006—Laurie Richardson, Henderson, Nevada. (*Church News*, 5/13/06)

2005—Helen Bean, Oregon City, Oregon. (*The Oregonian*, 5/2/05)

FILE PHOTO
Helen Bean

Miss Junior Teen
2003—Kristen Tanner, 15, El Centro Ward, Sacramento California North Stake (*Church News*, 4/3/04)

Miss Yakima Nation
1979—Judy Neaman, Zillah Ward, Yakima Washington Stake (Odessa Johnson, 1/31/05)

OUTSTANDING TEEN DANCER. Garrett Smith, 17, Copperview 2nd Ward, Riverton Utah Copperview Stake, discovered at age 2 that he was a very natural athlete and dancer, and won the 2006 Outstanding Teen Male Dancer for the New York City Dance Alliance. The prior year he won Outstanding Junior dancer by the same alliance, making him the only dancer ever to win back-to-back championships. (*Church News*, 4/29/06)

TELEVISION

FIRST DOCUMENTARY ON LATTER-DAY SAINTS IN ROMANIA. After 45 years of communist control, Romania finally became a free nation in 1989. The next year, LDS missionaries were sent to begin spreading the gospel message. From that time forward, numerous anti-Mormon propaganda pieces and reports were disseminated throughout the country, and the missionary work suffered as a result. And then along came Daniel Hintergraber in 2003. He was a university student in Bucharest studying televi-

Daniel Hintergraber introduced the Church to a reluctant Romania and made a huge difference in the missionary work and good will.

DANIEL HINTERGRABER

sion and movie making when he joined the Church. In 2004, Brother Hintergraber decided to create a short TV special to promote the Church. He had action clips of the Joseph Smith story reenacted and had them shown on the local television station in Bucharest. Later he traveled to Utah to do a more in-depth documentary on the Church. His visit took him through Salt Lake City, the Missionary Training Center in Provo, and to the homes of parents of a few of the missionaries who were serving in Romania. He also filmed Romanian members of the Church involved in positive activities right there in Romania. The footage turned into seven separate television specials, each narrated by Brother Hintergraber. After the programs were aired, local missionaries reported their work became much more successful, and the Church continues to grow. (Darrell Weber, 3/30/06)

FILE PHOTO

Ken Jennings ultimately won $2,520,700 from JEOPARDY! Look for his fascinating new book, *Brainiac*.

MOST MONEY WON BY A LATTER-DAY SAINT ON A TV GAME SHOW. In June 2004, Ken Jennings, 30, of Murray, Utah, shattered records for JEOPARDY!, a quiz show in which an answer is given and the contestant must provide the question. Brother Jennings, a returned missionary from Madrid, defended his championship for 74 consecutive games and won $2,520,700. He gave more than 2,700 correct responses on subjects from Shakespeare to hiphop. Game show host Alex Trebek said, "I very much doubt that we will ever see an accomplishment like this again. Ken is a one of a kind." During Brother Jennings appearances, ratings for JEOPARDY! averaged 22 percent higher. In the 75th game, the answer was, "Most of this firm's 70,000 seasonal white-collar employees work only four months a year." The correct question was, "What is HandR Block?" but Brother Jennings said, "What is FedEx?" His nationwide fame led to appearances on all of the major talk shows and radio and television for weeks afterward. He has since written a book (*Brainiac, Adventures in the Curious, Competitive, Compulsive World of Trivia Buffs*), developed a board game called "Can You Beat Ken?" and made various contributions to children's teaching aids and other published works and columns. (www.ken-jennings.com; www.jeopardy.com; *Church News*, 12/4/04)

BEST LDS LIAR ON A TV GAME SHOW. In 2002, the TV game show *To Tell the Truth* was into its 46th year on television and was syndicated to various networks and stations across America. That's when Eric Strassforth, Ventura 2nd Ward, Ventura California Stake, walked onto the stage. It was Brother Strassforth's job to fool everybody that he was the real contestant, a man named Joe Kelly who founded Dads and Daughters, and also shared the stage. As the questioning progressed, the panelists asked about father-daughter relationships, the negative influence of Britney Spears, and more. At the conclusion, each celebrity exclaimed how they were touched and moved by "Number Two's" (Strassforth's) answers. In fact, all four voted for him as did a full 62 percent of the audience. When moderator John O'Hurley stated those famous lines, "Will the real Joe Kelly please stand up?" it was not Number Two who stood, but Number One, the real Joe Kelly. The entire audience erupted in a standing ovation, not just for the positive works of the real Joe Kelly, but for the sincerity, persuasiveness, and genuine demeanor of Strassforth. "I was able to meet the celebrities for about 20 seconds after the show," Strassforth said. "The panelists were really angry at me at the end. I had fooled them all. But my fellow contestants and I ended up with $1,667 each, which of course was the most you could win." (Author interview, 4/5/06)

STAR ON HOLLYWOOD WALK OF FAME. Art Acord, Prattsville, Utah, has been honored with a star on the Hollywood Walk of Fame. He was a silent movie star in Hollywood and was known as the Mormon Cowboy. He was a rodeo champion and won the World Steer Wrestling Championship in 1912 and 1916. (John Bascom, 5/15/06)

Other LDS Stars on the Hollywood Walk of Fame. The master record includes the following Latter-day Saints honored in famous Hollywood cement:

> Billy Barty
> The Osmond Family
> Glen Larson
> Rhonda Fleming
> Robert Walker
> Marie Windsor
> Joi Lansing
> Fay Wray (Ethnic Mormon—raised by non-practicing Latter-day
>   Saints, not baptized)
> Mack Swain
> Terry Moore

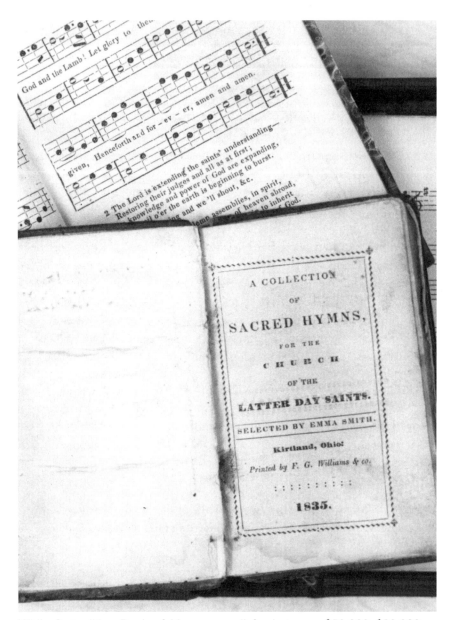

While first-edition Book of Mormons sell for between $50,000–$80,000 or more, who would have guessed that a mint condition copy of Emma Smith's 1835 hymnal would one day auction for $273,600? The 2006 sale was believed to be the third highest price ever paid for an LDS book. Christie's Auction House did the preliminary research and found that only two other copies of the hymnal on record—both imperfect and one very defective. The buyer and seller in the transaction were both kept confidential, although the seller said the book was "property of a gentleman."

PUBLISHING

MORMON ACHIEVEMENTS BY THE NUMBERS

3—Beach Boys who received a copy of the Book of Mormon
35—Nations beat by BYU marketing team in a worldwide competition
120,000,000—Copies of the Book of Mormon printed since 1830

THE BOOK OF MORMON

NOW YOU KNOW: For the two or three people arguing over the correct plural form for the Book of Mormon, here's the answer. Some people believe it should be "Books of Mormon"; others subscribe to "Book of Mormons." The term "Books of Mormon" literally means many books from or belonging to the ancient American prophet Mormon. Using "Book of Mormons" is the correct form to describe many copies of the Book of Mormon. If the arguing between your neighborhood grammarians has turned to throwing copies of the *Ensign* at each other, calm it down with this handy default: "Copies of the Book of Mormon."

MOST CONTROVERSIAL CHANGE. For the second edition of the "reader friendly" edition of the Book of Mormon published by Doubleday in October 2006, the Church made a slight word change in the introduction. The old phrase used to say that the Lamanites "are the principle ancestors of the American Indians." The new phrase says that the Lamanites "are among the ancestors of the American Indians." The original introduction was not part of the Joseph Smith translation and was written for the 1981 version of the book. The change de-emphasizes a connection between the American Indians and the Lamanites, who are of Middle Eastern origin. This stirred controversy after DNA analysis found little connection between American Indians and those of Middle Eastern descent. Give it a break, guys; sign seeking doesn't pay. (*Deseret News*, 11/8/07)

BOOK OF MORMONS GIVEN TO FAMOUS PEOPLE. In the ongoing work to share the great gospel message with others, copies of the Book of Mormon have been patient missionaries, finding their way into libraries, hotels, waiting rooms, and even among the rich and famous. Here is the latest batch of Book of Mormon missionary stories.

FILE PHOTO

Neil Diamond said, "Trajan, I'm a Jew!" to which Brother Weaver responded, "Right! It was written for the Jew, that's YOU!"

Neil Diamond. When the world-famous singer/songwriter Neil Diamond was in Salt Lake City in November 2005 for a concert, he met up with Trajan Weaver, a member of the Church living south of the city. Trajan's family is very well known. His father, Pat Weaver, was considered one of the founding fathers of television who helped break the "one-sponsor" trend carried over from the old radio days. Pat (not a member) also started *The Today Show*, *The Tonight Show*, *The Home Show*, and dozens of other innovations. Trajan's famous sister, Sigourney Weaver, has starred in the famous *Alien* science fiction movies, as well as the First Lady in *Dave*, the token blonde bombshell in *Galaxy Quest*, and a host of others. Because of Sigourney's friendship with Neil Diamond, Trajan was given front row tickets to Diamond's concert in the Salt Palace. After the show, Trajan met the singer in his dressing room to say hello and deliver a copy of the Book of Mormon. "But I'm a Jew," Neil Diamond said with a smile. "That's exactly right," Trajan said. "See? It says right here in the front, 'written for the Jew,' that's YOU, and 'written for the gentile,' that's ME!" Diamond took the book with a smile and a handshake. (Author's interview)

FILE PHOTO

Al Sharpton took some valuable time to fly to Salt Lake City and learn about the Church to which presidential hopeful Mitt Romney adhered. He left as a new and informed friend.

Al Sharpton. In the heat of political debate regarding Latter-day Saint Mitt Romney's run for president, Reverend Al Sharpton made a statement that was construed by some as offensive to Mormons. To demonstrate that his comments were directed at an atheist and not Mormons, Reverend Sharpton made a trip to Salt Lake City to apologize for any misunderstanding and to learn more about the Church and its beliefs. He was hosted by Elder Robert C. Oaks and Elder M. Russell Ballard for a tour of Temple Square, Church headquarters, Welfare Square, the Family History Library, the Conference Center, the Tabernacle, and a Monday-night family home evening at the home of Jorge and Debbie Becerra in Salt Lake City. Before his departure, he was presented with a copy of the Book of Mormon by Elder Ballard. (LDS.org Newsroom, 5/22/07; LDS Public Affairs Department)

The Beach Boys/Murray Wilson. The world-famous Beach Boys received one of their first big pushes in Utah. Bill Hesterman, station manager of the most-listened-to music radio station at the time, 1280 AM, KNAK in Salt Lake City, Utah, helped "discover" the Beach Boys. It was common for him to receive many promo records from producers, and when the Beach Boys' single arrived, he gave it a spin and liked what he heard. Over time he built a good friendship with the group's father, Murray Wilson (father of Dennis, Brian, and Carl, and group manager). Brother Hesterman invited the Beach Boys to Utah to perform at Lagoon and other venues. As the group's popularity grew, so did Brother Hesterman's involvement, and he joined them on a tour to Europe in 1964. Hesterman's wife, Barbara, says that her husband took over a briefcase of Book of Mormons and handed them out everywhere he could, including to Murray Wilson. Nothing more came of it, Sister Hesterman said, except a few years later from a band member who had dropped out in the early years, Al Jardine. After purchasing a non-working ranch, he called the Hestermans one evening. "Guess what I've got going on in my barn tonight?" he asked. They just shrugged, "We have no idea!" "Your Church

FILE PHOTO

This may be the "lost photo" of the Beach Boys with Mike Love (third from left) looking away. On the 1967 marketed album he's looking at the camera. Next to him in the black trousers is LDS Bishop Bill Hesterman, the DJ who helped launch the career of the Beach Boys. This photo is taken with the old Saltaire pavilion in the background at the Great Salt Lake.

is doing a road show in my barn!" (Interview with Barbara Hesterman, 6/20/07)

Other famous recipients of the Book of Mormon contained in the master record:

Abraham Lincoln
Ronald Reagan
U.S. Senator Ted Kennedy
Queen Victoria
Muhammad Ali
John F. Kennedy
Mark Twain
Nikita Khrushchev's family
Winston Churchill
Elvis Presley
Leo Tolstoy
Sgt. Alvin C. York
Coretta Scott King
Jesse Jackson
Peggy Fleming
. . . and others

BYU NEWSNET

Zack Tolbert, Jamie Bond, and Stanton Jones won the 2007 L'Oreal Brandstorm Best Communications Campaign Award in Paris

MARKETING

BEST COMMUNICATORS. In June 2007, three BYU students swept the annual Brandstorm marketing competition held in Paris and sponsored by L'Oreal. Stanton Jones, Jamie Bond, and Zack Tolbert out-created the top advertising students from 35 nations in this prestigious worldwide competition. Ad Lab faculty advisor Jeff Sheets was also on hand for the honors. The trio became the official representatives of the U.S. after defeating 200 others teams from across America at the national Brandstorm in New York. L'Oreal's Francois de Wazieres said the BYU team's "energy, passion and drive tied with their strong background in advertising led them to take this year's U.S. competition." In one phase of the competition, the team took female ad professionals from L'Oreal's advertising agency into an empty men's room so the ladies could appreciate the uncomfortable feeling men have in beauty salons, and while there they presented ideas on a men's salon design. While other teams partied in the City of Lights, the BYU team stuck to school and Church standards and focused on the task at hand, leaving the touring until after the contest ended. (BYU NewsNet, 6/25/07; photo by Jeff Sheets)

JOHN BRUCE

John Bruce, Draper 12th Ward, Draper Utah Stake, begins some repair work on his 700-pound masterpiece, an 8-foot tall, 32-inch in diameter, larger-than-life nutcracker, created from one piece of fallen spruce. The piece was originally created in 1978, sold a few times, stolen, and finally recovered and sold again to a buyer in Seattle. Brother Bruce is one of many LDS craftsmen and artists whose works adorn the world of music, art, and photography.

MUSIC, ART, and PHOTOGRAPHY

MORMON ACHIEVEMENTS BY THE NUMBERS

3—Oboists in one LDS family

97—Age of the oldest living Tabernacle Choir member

220—Feet wide for world's largest mural

12,500,000—Printed postage stamps designed by a Latter-day Saint

MUSIC

COMPOSER OF DISNEY'S BEST. Leigh Harline (3/26/1907– 12/10/1969) was born in Salt Lake City and was one of 13 children. He joined the Disney studios in 1932 as an arranger and scorer. He wrote the music for "When You Wish Upon A Star," the classic that won the Academy Award for Best Original Song in 1940. He wrote other tunes familiar to tens of millions all around the world, including "I'm Wishing," "Whistle While You Work," "Heigh Ho," and "Some Day My Prince Will Come." His musical talents were shared in at least 146 movies, many uncredited—among those is *It's A Won-*

FILE PHOTO

When Leigh Harline wished upon a star, he won an Oscar.

derful Life. Brother Harline was also the first Latter-day Saint to win an Academy Award. He was honored with an Oscar for Best Musical Score for Disney's *Pinocchio* in 1940. (Online biography)

THE LETTERMEN. Founded by Latter-day Saint Jim Pike and later joined by his brother Gary Pike, The Lettermen had 46 consecutive hit record albums, 20 hit singles, nine gold record albums, five Grammy nominations, and with record, tape, and CD sales, more than $100 million worldwide. In October 2001, Jim and Gary were inducted into the Vocal Group Hall of Fame as "The Lettermen." They appeared in shows such as *Red Skeleton, Dick Clark,*

FILE PHOTO

WWW.JIMPIKE.NET

Ric de Azevedo and Jim and Gary Pike bring The Lettermen hits to life in their new group, Reunion, that was formed in 1983 and performs to sold-out audiences even today.

The Tonight Show, the Miss Universe and Miss America pageants, as well as more appearances on the *Ed Sullivan Show* than any other musical group. Some of their hit songs include "The Way You Look Tonight," "When I Fall In Love," "Put Your Head On My Shoulder," "I Only Have Eyes For You," among others. They even left an impression on the moon when NASA included The Lettermen's hit song, "Love," in a time capsule left by Apollo Astronauts. In the late 1960s, Jim Pike developed a medical problem in his throat that ended his professional singing career, and he sold The Lettermen to Tony Butala, the third member of the trio. Ten years later, Jim was asked to be in a bishopric in California. The stake president told him if he accepted the calling he would be able to sing again. Jim took the position and is again singing with his brother Gary and Ric de Azevedo, in their new group, Reunion. According to *Billboard* magazine, Jim and Gary's former group was referred to as "The Greatest Romantic Vocal Group of All Time!" (Brent Ayre, 02/10/06 and www.jimpike.net)

LARGEST GUITAR JAM (1994 WORLDS RECORD). On May 7, 1994, Latter-day Saint Randy Bachman (Guess Who, BTO), led 1,322 mostly amateur guitarists in a mass guitar jam session in Vancouver, British Columbia, that lasted 68 minutes.

SHIRLEY ENGLAND

Shirley Johnson at the time she had fun, fun, fun till her daddy took the T-bird away.

MOST FAMOUS BEACH BOYS' SONG. It was 1964, and teenager Shirley Johnson (Johnson is her maiden name) wanted to meet up with her friends at Shoor's Drive-In for some food and talk. The drive out to 33rd South and 27th East in Salt Lake City in her dad's new Thunderbird should have been a short enough trip for burgers and a shake, but it was her excuse that caused all the problems. She told her father, Howard D. Johnson, that she was headed to the library. Unfortunately, the library closed at nine, and she didn't get home until after ten. The late arrival resulted in her being grounded and the keys to

Dad's car taken away. The rest of the story revolves around Howard Johnson's popular radio station, 1280 AM KNAK, in Salt Lake City, Utah. The station manager was Bill Hesterman, who happened to be friends with a California man named Murray Wilson, whose three boys were starting up a band with their cousin. When the band's promo record arrived at KNAK, Brother Hesterman threw it on just for kicks. The sound was good. He liked it. And from that point forward, he promoted the young boys and their new musical sound. So, back to Shirley Johnson—the following day, after the "dad and car incident," she showed up at her father's radio station, where she worked part-time. She was still smarting from the loss of access to Dad's car. In studio that day were the Wilson boys doing an on-air interview. She told everyone about her woes, and the boys joined in the teasing that she shouldn't try to hide things from her dad. Later

FILE PHOTO

Bishop Bill Hesterman's friendship and help in launching the Beach Boys' career was honored with his appearance on this 1967 album cover. This photo was taken at the old Saltaire on the shores of the Great Salt Lake.

FILE PHOTO

Bill Hesterman joins the touring Beach Boys on stage for some sing-a-longs and reminiscing with his old friends.

that day, Brother Hesterman took the boys back to the airport in his Cadillac. During the ride, they were talking and laughing about Shirley's tale of misery and then started to toy around with the story. Key words came out like *T-bird* (Dad's car), *hamburger stand*, *library*, and the most famous of all, *fun, fun, fun*! By the time they pulled up at the airport, they had the lyrics to a super-hit, "Fun, Fun, Fun!" and put it on their 1964 album, *The Beach Boys: Shut Down, Volume 2*. The rest is history!

The first verse:

Well she got her daddy's car
And she cruised through the hamburger stand now
Seems she forgot all about the library
Like she told her old man now
And with the radio blasting
Goes cruising just as fast as she can now
And she'll have fun fun fun
'Til her daddy takes the T-Bird away
(Fun fun fun 'til her daddy takes the T-Bird away)
(Lyrics © The Beach Boys)

SHIRLEY ENGLAND

Shirley Johnson England poses in front of a vintage Thunderbird (T-Bird) with a framed 45 of the famous Beach Boys hit that she inspired.

(Source: Interview with Shirley Johnson England, Brighton Point Ward, Salt Lake City Utah Butler Stake, and Barbara Hesterman, Murray 24th Ward, Murray Utah Stake, 6/20/07)

WORLD RENOWNED PIANIST. Pianist Grant Johannesen has been called one of the finest musicians that ever achieved international fame to come from Utah.

Brother Johannesen was born in Salt Lake City in 1921. His musical skill on the piano was discovered when a neighbor piano teacher heard him imitating her performance at the age of 5. As the years passed, he studied with Robert Casadesus, Roger Sessions, and Nadia Boulanger. He performed at Times Hall and toured Europe for two years with the New York Philharmonic, and later toured Europe and the USSR with the Cleveland Orchestra under George Szell. On one tour in Moscow, Russia, he was encored 16 times, and for his last encore he performed "Come, Come Ye Saints." He regularly performed in concerts and festivals in the U.S. and Europe, and was best known for his interpretation of French composers. Brother Johannesen passed away in 2005 at age 83. (*Deseret News*, 3/29/05)

FILE PHOTO

Book cover. Grant Johannesen completed his memoirs shortly before his death in 2005.

WORLD'S BEST A CAPPELLA. April 29, 2006, was unusual because for years, the International Championship of Collegiate A Cappella finals were always held on Sunday, and no matter how far BYU teams finished in the finals, they could never compete for the championship. But in 2006, the competition was changed to a Saturday and BYU's male group "Vocal Point" swept the competition and took first place. And consider-

BYU NEWSNET

In 2006, BYU's "Vocal Point" took first place over the regional champs from across the U.S., Canada, and Western Europe.

ing their competition makes the win that much more amazing. Second place went to Oxford University's Out of the Blue, and third place went to University of Illinois's The Other Guys. "We were just thrilled to make it here," said Jordan Keith of Vocal Point. The group performed before a sold-out Lincoln Center audience in New York. They were first up—a dangerous spot because judges tend to forget the earliest acts. But their 12-minute presentation wowed them all. They opened with a vocal rendition of the famous "THX Sound Effect" that is presented at the opening of many movies, and followed that with the famous "20th Century Fox Theme." This was followed by the *Spider-Man* theme, "He Is Born," and the jazz piece "Sing, Sing, Sing." The group was organized in 1991 and performs everywhere. (*Meridian Magazine*; *Deseret News*, 5/3/06; *Daily Herald*, 5/3/06)

NELSON FAMILY

It's not uncommon in a family to have multiple piano or violin players, but when it comes to the difficult but beautifully toned oboe, nobody beats this Nelson trio (l-r): Kellie, Kasey and Nathanael.

MOST OBOISTS—ONE FAMILY. It's an unusual gift to play the double reed, but in the Nelson family of six, the three eldest children are budding masters on the oboe. Kasey, 16, picked it up in the third grade and thought at the time "it was the coolest thing in the world! It is a beautiful instrument to play and very unique, which gives me more of a chance to shine when I play instead of blending in with the larger sections." Her sister Kellie, 12, plays oboe in her elementary school. "I chose oboe because my older sister plays it and I could get more sound out of the oboe than any other instrument." Younger brother Nathanael, 9, chose the oboe because his sisters were doing so well with it, but also because "some kids call it loud and screechy, and say it sounds like a dying duck." Sister Barbara Nelson reports the children are each excelling and the talent may lead them to music majors in college. (Author interview, 2/16/07)

DARTH VADER VIOLIN. He may be the villain of the ever-enduring *Star Wars* movie sequels, but there's no "dark side of the force" emanating from Elder Timothy O'Brien's violin when he performs. This unique carving came compliments of a local member in Elder O'Brien's mission in Bolivia who was skilled in the art and created perhaps the only one of its kind in the world—or at least the Church. No doubt Darth and the Elder make beautiful music together. (Timothy O'Brien)

The Suzuki-Vader Method? No, it's just a very talented LDS violin maker and wood carver in Bolivia giving Elder O'Brien a stringed version of The Force.

TIM O'BRIEN

YOUNGEST ORGANIST. They called them pretty young back in the day, but when that was the only talent on hand, it became no doubt a fantastic growing experience for these young musicians.

In 1927, Nadine Diffey (Bascom) was the youngest organist sustained and set apart for the Raytown Mississippi Branch at the age of 11. She played the pump organ for regular Church services, for the choir, for area conferences where Apostle Charles A. Calis presided, and for dances and funerals. Her amazing talent was that she never took a music lesson but played by ear on both piano and organ. In 1936 she met rodeo cowboy Earl Bascom in church in Columbia, and after her mission to Georgia, the two were married in the Salt Lake Temple in 1939. In her 90s, she continued to perform, playing a washboard in her local pioneer band. (John Bascom, 4/17/2006)

In 1969, Brian Ballard was the official youngest organist in a ward at the age of 12. "I was so short, I couldn't reach the pedals," he said. But that didn't stop him from playing for every auxiliary organization in his ward, including the Relief Society. Back then he served in the California Walnut Creek Stake, but today resides in the Taylorsville 24th Ward, Taylorsville Utah Stake. (Brian Ballard, 2/26/05)

TABERNACLE CHOIR

OLDEST TABERNACLE CHOIR MEMBER. In 2004, 97-year-old Margarete Stahl Wilken Hicken was honored as the oldest living member of the Tabernacle Choir. She joined the choir in 1929, and though she didn't sing in the first broadcast, she was present for the centennial celebration of the Church in 1930. After her marriage in the late 1930s, she retired from the choir and became an avid listener and watcher. (www.mormontabernaclechoir.org)

WWW.MORMONTABERNACLECHOIR.ORG

Margarete Hicken enjoys a visit with Craig Jessop (l) and CBU radio commentator Charles Osgood during an event honoring her service and longevity.

MOST FAMILY PARTICIPATION IN TABERNACLE CHOIR. An enjoyable family legacy involving the Mormon Tabernacle Choir recently reached another milestone. In 2004, Sarah Clayton joined the Choir and became the

SUSAN CLAYTON

The current generation of Susan and Sarah Clayton's relatives in the Tabernacle Choir and Orchestra include: Front row: Ann Clark Ashton, Jane Hillier Clark, Sarah Clayton; Back Row: Kim Cheshire, Shane Clark, Elliott Clark, and Susan Hillier Clayton.

first in her family's sixth consecutive generation to sing in the famed group. She joined her mother, Susan Hillier Clayton, who was already a member. Sarah's grandmother, Helen Russell Hillier, had been a member, as was her great-grandfather Valoran Russell. The other two generations are represented by her great-great-grandmother, Hedvig "Hattie" Aurora Lundgren Dahl and great-great-great-grandmother, Alma Elizabeth "Lizzie" Mineer Felt, who first joined the Choir in 1883. The family talent for beautiful music extends beyond that direct family line. The family has had 30 members in the choir, and ten family members at one time in the 1970s and seven family members at one time since the year 2000. Others have also performed for the Orchestra at Temple Square and Temple Square Chorale. (Author's interview, 9/23/04)

FIRST AND ONLY TABERNACLE CHOIR MATCHMAKING? For Ken and Marybeth Wynder, now of the Bountiful 4th Ward, Mueller Park Utah Stake, singing in the Tabernacle Choir became "a once in a lifetime" experience of a different sort. When the two first joined in 1975, they eventually met each other, started dating, fell in love, and got married on August 15, 1975. They wondered, what to do for the honeymoon? As it turned out, the Choir was scheduled for a Canadian tour just three days later, so the Wynders invited their 350 choir friends to join them on their honeymoon. Jump ahead 20 years to their mandatory retirement date, and the two left the choir on the same day. The love story was shared nationwide by radio celebrity Paul Harvey, who told his nationwide audience the happy story of a young couple literally making beautiful music together. (Author's interview, 1/26/05)

FIRST NON-CATHOLIC CHOIR IN NOTRE DAME. Brother Ralph Woodward, Edgemont Utah Stake, was a gifted music school professor at BYU. He led the school to become one of the preeminent music schools in the U.S. His crowning achievement at the Y was the BYU A Cappella Choir which, among its many honors and achievements, was also the first non-Roman Catholic choir to sing in the Notre Dame Cathedral in Paris three times. Brother Woodward was listed in *Who's Who in Music* and *Who's Who in the West*, and became internationally respected for his outstanding leadership and achievements. (*Deseret News,* 9/8/05)

PAINTING

WORLD'S LARGEST MURAL (2004 WORLD RECORD). At the south end of Gillette, Wyoming, is a huge warehouse that previously served as a dry dock enclosure on the Great Lakes. Standing alone at its new home in the wind-swept desert, it seemed so out of place that its owners commissioned professional painter Harvey Jackson of Gillette, Wyoming, to help spruce it up. Jackson proposed a massive mural along one side that depicted scenes of the West, both old and new, including long-haul trucks, train, cattle, and more. They liked his ideas and budgeted $290,000 for materials, engineering help, labor, and supplies. Jackson set up shop in a nearby warehouse and started wrestling with how to paint the side of the 60-foot tall building in windy weather that wasn't cooperative. Jackson decided to create the huge mural indoors by painting portions of it onto individual galvanized steel panels, each measuring 4 x 10 feet and weighing 110 pounds. He would attach these on the exterior of the building, and if all went well, they would blend together like a giant jigsaw puzzle. The finished product took 286 panels. To correctly draw out the mural a tiny piece at a time, he mapped the shapes and lines onto each panel using his computer. But painting those himself would have taken years, so he enlisted the help of 250 local at-risk

L&H INDUSTRIES

Harvey Jackson's giant mural covering the side of the center building is almost 60 feet tall and 220 feet long. Laid on the ground, it would cover most of a football field.

MARC ROCHKIND, WWW.BASEPATH.COM

A close-up view of the mural gives some perspective of its larger-than-life size.

kids. Each morning, Jackson would arrive early to paint black lines on the panels and number the spaces to indicate which color went into which area. When the kids arrived, he put them to work using 3- and 4-inch brushes to apply the paint. They used 150 colors and 220 gallons of paint that were all mixed on site. The paint was a special non-fade, exterior mixture that added $10,000 to the project's cost. Jackson spent an entire year planning the project, two months to paint the panels and four months to do touch-up work. He used a cherry-picker type crane to install the panels and secured them in place with at least 40 screws per panel—that's more than 11,000 screws. At times he was 60 feet in the air wrestling a heavy panel against wind and a swaying crane—not your average day for most artists. The finished product was 220 feet wide and 56 feet tall. To get an idea of the huge size of the subjects painted, the eye of one of the cows takes one whole panel, and the cow itself is larger than the head of George Washington on Mount Rushmore. He also included a life-size long-haul truck and a train that measured 60 feet by 59 feet. The mural is so large that visitors can see it from four miles away, day and night. Are there plans for more like this? "Absolutely!" Jackson said. "Just give me a call!" (Author's interview, 11/4/04)

ARTISTS, COMIC BOOKS, OTHER

YOUNG FAMILY

YOUNGEST STAMP DESIGNER. On August 22, 1999, Ashley M. Young, Glacial Park Ward, Sandy Utah Granite View Stake, became one of four representatives from the U.S. at the Universal Postal Congress in Beijing, China, where her winning design was selected from those of 120,000 other U.S. entries and countless thousands from around the world. Ashley portrayed a dog in a space helmet to represent an ideal future when even our pets can join us in space. Ashley is the daughter of Kurt O. and Lisa A. Young, and said, "My mom gave me an entrance form for an art contest, and I came up with the idea to paint a dog in outer space who I [named] Fetch." In July 2000, some 12,500,000 stamps featuring Ashley's artwork were issued. For her winning design she also won a computer, printer, software, and all-expense paid trips to New York and California. Ashley went on to pursue visual arts in college. (Author's interview, 3/31/05)

FILE PHOTO

FIRST LDS TRADING CARDS. In 2004, Arthur Nelson and Stephen Nelson published the first "Spirit Heroes" Book of Mormon trading cards. Their initial run of 74 characters from the Book of Mormon featured a full-color characterization of the individual on the front of the card and a brief biography with references to their story on the back. (Author's interview, 12/10/04)

FIRST BOOK OF MORMON COMIC BOOK. When Michael Allred's project for industry-leader Marvel Comics was cancelled, he felt the time was right to finish up a daring idea of his—the Book of Mormon comic book. His

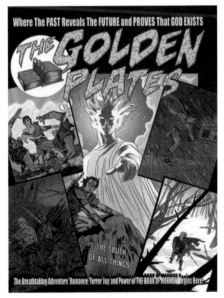

dream project unfolded under the title of *The Golden Plates: The Sword of Laban and the Tree of Life.* This was the first of a dozen other comic books he had planned, 64 pages each and full color. Brother Allred wrote, illustrated, and lettered the comics that present in a very sober and authentic manner the drama and adventure surrounding the Book of Mormon and related events. And he's no amateur, having 15 years of work for comic giants such as Marvel and DC Comics, where he drew many famous characters, including Spider-Man and the X-Men series.

After the first three weeks, Brother Allred's *Golden Plates* comic book had sold more than 12,000 copies. He and his wife and children live in Lakeside, Oregon. (*Salt Lake Tribune*, 11/26/04; *Deseret News*, 11/1/04)

> Other LDS comic strip artists listed in the master record:
> Ric Estrada—Superman (comic book)
> Brian Crane—Pickles (newspaper)
> Kevin Fagan—Drabble (newspaper)
> Richard Comely—Captain Canuck (comic book)
> Sal Velluto—Major artist for D.C. Comics and Marvel Comics

SCULPTURE ART

MOST FAMOUS LDS JEWELRY. It began innocently enough. The sisters on that early 1960s Primary General Board committee were looking for some way to help children to remember Jesus and do what was right. From that beginning came the slogan, "Choose the Right," and its initials on a shield with a green background. Primary children first saw it on their new 1963 Primary manual. By 1970, the idea was put on an expandable band ring. The new CTR ring adorned at least 10,000 little fingers for weeks before turning them all black. The manufacturer replaced them at no charge, using another metal that would not react to the skin in that way. While CTR was introduced as "Choose the Right," alternatives have emerged over the years such as "Current Temple Recommend" and in reverse, "Remember the Covenants." Literally millions of CTR rings have been distributed around the world since those early days. More than half a million in more than 30 languages are distributed annually. Prices have range from $.30 to $200, and the familiar shield can be found in tie tacks, jewelry, balloons, T-shirts, belt buckles, ties, scarfs, stationery, jackets, and more. The Church owns the copyright on the CTR emblem. The names associated with the ring idea and the committee and manufacturers include Church committee member Helen Alldredge (died September 28, 2006, age 93), com-

FILE PHOTO

One of the popular Mormonads from the July 2000 *New Era* magazine.

mittee member Naomi W. Randall (died May 17, 2001, age 92), committee member Norma Olsen Nichols (died October 2, 2004, age 94), committee member Lurene Wilkinson, ring fabricator Douglas "Coy" Miles, and fabrication designer Joel Izatt. (*Salt Lake Tribune*, 10/6/06, 11/04/07; *Church News*, 10/17/98, 10/3/04)

LARGEST CARVED BEAR. In 1998, James R. Veater, a high priest in the Jordan River Ridge 3rd Ward, River Ridge Utah Stake, carved a life-sized grizzly bear from a couple of old cottonwood stumps he found in Riverton, Utah. He first made a small clay model and created drawings from various angles to keep the carving in line. Three months and three electric chain saws later, his finished bear was ready for the final touches. He used a torch to darken the wood, and an electric chisel to detail the face, and a little sanding on the nose and eyes. Some linseed oil and a little stain was the finishing touch. The life-sized grizzly stands nine feet tall and averages 34 inches in diameter. Brother Veater estimates he put in about 300 hours. For

PAUL B. SKOUSEN

Trick or Treat! James Veater's giant bear stands nine feet tall. Elisabeth Skousen poses next to "Balou" to give some perspective on the bear's mammoth life-sized bulk.

local ward members, it's the prime landmark among homes, and a frequent photo shoot for students from the local high school learning about photography. Little kids were scared at first, Brother Veater said, but over time their concern turned to amazement. "We call it Balou," he said. The bear stands outside, and so far people have been respectable of it. "We've found him diapered with toilet paper on two occasions, but otherwise, they just enjoy looking." (Author's interview, 10/10/04)

LARGEST CARVED NUTCRACK-ER. In 1978, John Bruce, Draper 12th Ward, Draper Utah Stake, put the finishing touches on his 700-pound masterpiece, an 8-foot tall, 32-inch in diameter, larger-than-life nutcracker, all from one piece of fallen spruce. His only tools were mallets and chisels—no electric tools at all. The Scrooge nutcracker was his largest ever, and a uniquely designed masterpiece that he sold to a doctor in Utah County. The Scrooge later changed hands several times, fell into disrepair, and was then stolen. Brother Bruce finally located it and bought it back. After some repairs he sold it again to a buyer in Washington state, where it proudly stands today.

Nutcrackers have been a major theme of Brother Bruce's works over the years, part of a portfolio of

JOHN BRUCE

John Bruce works on his 8-foot-tall nutcracker, using only a mallet and chisels. Electric sanders helped with the finish work, but no other electric tools were used.

JOHN BRUCE

John Bruce has crafted wooden nutcrackers that are larger than life (left), or flatter than cardboard (right). And all of them work. The flat version pictured here measures 3-1/2" x 5" and has moving parts.

JOHN BRUCE

amazing carvings and creations that number in the thousands. Brother Bruce has plans to build the world's largest nutcracker (more than 16 feet tall) and hopes to start the project in the near future. (Author's interview, 11/11/04)

SMALLEST CARVED NUTCRACKER. John Bruce, of the Draper 12th Ward, Draper Utah Stake, fashioned his "magnus minimus" in the form of a tiny nutcracker painstakingly carved into the end of a wooden matchstick. It actually works, although even the experts are puzzled as to what size nuts such a nut cracker could handle. A second miniature that is much more detailed hardly spans the width of a thumbnail in overall length. At only 7/8-inch tall, his "Little Scrooge" was sold to a collector in the early 1980s. (Author's interview, 11/13/04)

JOHN BRUCE

"Little Scrooge" is good for cracking open those stubborn sesame seeds.

OTHER LDS SCULPTORS LISTED IN THE MASTER RECORD:

John Gutzon Borglum carved Mount Rushmore.

Avard Fairbanks' Angel Moroni design adorns LDS Temples.

Ed Fraughton Mormon Battalion figures are famous nationwide.

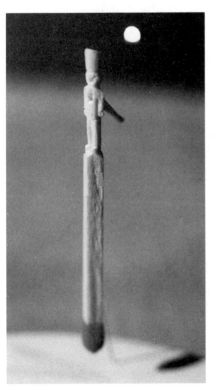

JOHN BRUCE

Got a light, buddy? The world's smallest hand-carved working nutcracker has only one major challenge: nuts small enough to prove itself in the storied world of nutcrackers!

USAF

Crash landing! In 1934 *Explorer I* ascended to a record altitude of 60,613 feet. Suddenly, the lower balloon seams ruptured and the craft began to plummet toward Earth. Without pressure suits, the three pilots had to wait for a lower altitude to bail out. Pictured in the lower right corner (tiny white oval), Latter-day Saint Orvil Anderson can be seen in his just-deployed parachute floating to safety.

COURAGE
MORMON ACHIEVEMENTS BY THE NUMBERS

220—Feet deep by an LDS deep-sea diver, a women's world record
100,000,000—Dollar value of land donated to the Church

RISKY EXPLORATION

HIGHEST BALLOON FLIGHTS (1934–35). It happened on a summer day of July 28, 1934. The Latter-day Saint about to make an ascent into the upper atmosphere by balloon didn't know he would also soon be taking a leap back out and down into the unknown. It was the free-fall of a lifetime.

Captain Orvil A. Anderson was born in Springville, Utah, on May 2, 1895, and attended local schools, including BYU. When World War I broke out, he enlisted in the army and made airships and ballooning his work and his hobby. The army sent him around the United States to help develop the newly emerging airship industry. His heroic handling of airships on experimental transcontinental flights when engine or weather problems forced landings, won him commendations from the chief of the Army Air Corps.

In 1934, Anderson was selected to pilot a balloon into the stratosphere. The massive balloon of rubberized canvas was inflated in a natural bowl-shaped depression near Rapid City, South Dakota, that was later named the Stratobowl. Cliffs rising 450 feet high surrounded the launchpad, helping to calm the winds that could wreak havoc on the buoyant balloons.

The balloon was called *Explorer I*, and was the largest constructed up to that time. It could hold 3 million cubic feet of hydrogen gas, and at ground level, only 250,000 cubic feet of gas was needed to inflate its hulk that towered more than 250 feet high (as tall as a 25-story building). At 6:45 AM on July 28, 1934, ground crews released the lines and the balloon began its rapid ascent into the still blue sky.

USAF

Explorer I rises above South Dakota on a calm, sunny day. It carried three passengers, two of them Latter-day Saints.

USAF

A bowl-shaped area in South Dakota became the launching point for upper atmosphere balloon flights. It was an ideal location because it protected the 30-story tall balloons from the wind.

During the flight, Captain Anderson and his two partners, Captain Albert W. Stevens and Major William E. Kepner, transmitted data and readings by radio to ground crews. Their living compartment was a welded and pressurized gondola 8-1/2 feet in diameter and painted white on the top and black on the bottom. The ascent was controlled by releasing gas at various intervals so temperature and pressure adjustments could be made. Inside the cramped quarters, the three aeronauts had instruments for conducting high-altitude tests and taking air samples.

All was going well until the balloon reached 60,613 feet—almost 11-1/2 miles up and within 624 feet of a new world altitude record. Suddenly, the worst of all possibilities broke loose: the bag began to rip. At this extreme altitude, the massive balloon that looked like a pudgy icicle at the start of its flight had now expanded to its full round size of 180 feet in diameter. Several small rips along seams began to enlarge and with gas hissing into the frigid upper atmosphere around them, the balloon began to drop. The ripping exposures frayed their way down the sides and opened into massive gaping holes that flapped slowly at it dropped into the thickening air. The balloon began to accelerate toward certain death some 10 miles below, and the men aboard hurried to prepare.

The aeronauts did not have pressure suits. This meant they couldn't open the gondola hatch until it was below 20,000 feet or the decreased pressure would cause them all to black out. Such occurrences had led to the deaths of other ballooning pioneers in prior years.

As their plummeting speed increased, huge sections of the balloon ripped off and drifted away. Only the top portion of the balloon remained intact, inflated like a parachute but doing little to slow the descent.

The men hurriedly strapped on their parachutes as the crippled craft dropped below the danger zone.

When they had passed through the 5,000-foot level, the remaining hydrogen mixed with oxygen at just the right proportion to suddenly explode, blowing apart more sections of the balloon. A shudder was felt through the craft, and the men knew that only seconds remained.

Finally, at 3,000 feet, the men forced the hatch open, and that's when Anderson realized his chute had come apart and was lying at his feet. He folded it over in his arms, shouted back to his comrades, "Well, it will either open or it won't," and leapt into the empty air. Fortunately, his chute did open and saved his life (see photograph).

Meanwhile, Captain Albert W. Stevens was having problems getting out. The screaming wind had slammed the hatch shut. At 2,000 feet, Stevens ran against the hatch, but the door wouldn't open. A second try and it threw open

SI Neg. # 97-15365

USAF MUSEUM

The pressurized gondola carried aloft by *Explorer I* disintegrated upon impact. The largest portion is pictured on the left. *Explorer II*'s gondola was lightened with half the equipment and only two crew members.

and he pushed off as hard as he could into the warming summer air. But that wasn't the end of his problems. Just after his chute opened, he was suddenly overshadowed by a massive sheet of the balloon's fabric that had blown off in the explosion. It enveloped him like the collapsing wings of a giant gray bird and crushed the air from his chute—but then it miraculously slid off at the very last second.

And at 500 feet, the last passenger, Major William E. Kepner, threw himself out, deployed his chute, and slowed just enough to step onto the ground that rushed up at him. All three watched in panicked relief as their life pod, that gondola and its many instruments, smashed into the ground like a raw egg and then was buried under by the heavy thud of ropes, steel cables, and mounds of shredded balloon fabric that lay in a dusty heap.

Fortunately, the men lived to fly another day— which they did the following year in *Explorer II*. (Ruth Stevens, "My Husband the First Astronaut," *The Improvement Era*, May 1936; *National Geographic*; various sources)

USAF

The *Explorer I* crew (l-r): Major William Kepner, Captain Albert Stevens, and Captain Orvil Anderson, on July 29, 1934. The *Explorer II* crew consisted of Stevens and Anderson.

The Hansens' Undersea Diving Catalina Calif.

BOB PLUNKETT

Norma Hanson prepares to drop into the water on her way to a depth of 220 feet, a new women's world record for deep-sea diving.

DEEPEST DEEP SEA DIVE—WOMEN (1950 WORLD RECORD). The life-threatening risks in deep-sea diving are numerous, and Norma Armour Hanson, Harbor 1st Ward, Palos Verdes California Stake, knows firsthand just how real those can be. With more than 4,000 dives under her belt, she was inducted into the Women's Diving Hall of Fame for being a pioneer in diving and opening the way for other women to follow.

On May 14, 1950, she set the women's world record for the deepest dive at 220 feet. "The trip down took only 10 minutes," she said. "But coming up took 2 hours and 40 minutes." The long ascent is for decompression purposes. "Take a bottle of soda pop and take the cap off and shake it up— that's the way your blood is when you go down. The air in your blood contracts, and the deeper you go, the smaller the bubbles get." She said if a diver rises too fast, the bubbles expand too fast, and it's lethal. But that's just one problem divers have to contend with!

An important part of diving is the tender, the team on the boat who times the ascent to prevent fatal decompression. At such deep levels, the air compressor topside must be able to force more air down the hoses to keep the diver alive. Rising to the surface, that compression is tapered off. For the first stop after her record dive, Norma was at 180 feet, where she had to wait for a full minute, and then her crew followed the Navy table for the rest of the ascent. At just 10 feet, that was the most critical point where she had to wait until the bubbles in her blood continued to shrink.

Communication between divers and those topside was

BOB PLUNKETT

Norma Hanson's record dive had a safety team, and a tender to run the pump, clear the lines, and maintain communication. Her husband, Al, was topside, making sure the dive went well.

made possible with a wired telephone system her husband, Alfred "Al" Hanson, developed, and being inside a large, round helmet breathing air or helium, he and Norma could stay in constant communication between each other and with the boat.

Sister Hanson was nearly always teamed with her husband. Together they took jobs inspecting piers, cleaning up around ships or shipwrecks, and performing for the famous glass-bottom boats off the coast of California's Catalina Island.

NORMA HANSON

Al Hanson prepares for a routine dive with Norma at the helm.

"Another problem is you sometimes get a little touch of narcosis," Sister Hanson said. Contracted one time to rig a ship that had sunk because it was overloaded with tuna, Al went down to around 200–250 feet. Norma was topside tending when he started laughing. "What are you doing?" she asked. Al just said, "Weeeeeeee, you can take these frozen albacore and shoot them and they come right back!" Norma knew there was a problem and began hoisting him back. "Al was mad as heck! He kept saying 'no, no, no, no!' but he was on the edge of blacking out, and part way up, he regained his senses and surfaced with a very sheepish look on his face. He apologized and knew what I had done—saved his life."

Sister Hanson says she and Al had all kinds of strange jobs. One job was fixing a broken sewer pipe that was spewing sewage into the ocean. "When Al came up, I hosed him off and washed his suit in the bathtub with good mild soap and then hung it up to dry. But in an oil spill, that's the worst thing because that clean up job can last for days . . . the hoses are covered in oil, the suits are covered head to foot, and it's hard to see the boat when you're coming up." She said after each oil-spill job they did, they had to buy new suits—at $1,000 per suit back in the 1950s.

The least little thing can create problems, Norma says. On one dive, at about 50 feet down, she felt a terrible burning feeling in one leg. It was a wrinkle in her long underwear, and the tremendous pressure compressing the suit against her skin created a really bad sore. But there were solutions, Norma said. "I'd let air fill up the suit and then go wiggle or grab something and go upside down, wriggle around to get the wrinkles out, flip back upright, get the air out of the suit, and keep going."

During one dive, a shark approached Norma. Her husband saw it first and called to her to watch out. "When that shark came up to within three feet of me, I kicked him in the teeth. I had never seen such a beautiful creature as it came swimming toward me. But when it opened its mouth, it was everyone's nightmare: I saw row after row after row of teeth! And he was fast. I mean, in just a flash he was there. When I got to the ladder, I could hold onto it, but out of the water I just couldn't stand on deck . . . I really and truly had rubber legs. That shark was 12 or 15 feet long—he looked like a miniature submarine! I've had a few nightmares over that shark. After that, when I went down, I was always glancing around."

Performing for the glass-bottom boats by feeding fish and walking on the sandy bottom wasn't the only performance the husband-wife team enjoyed. "We did everything and went everywhere, including stand-ins for several movies," Norma said. "I was the phantom in *The Phantom from 10,000 Leagues*, and I was the evil monster in the *Sea Gods of Shark Reef* and *International Warriors*. Those parts were really funny because the story wasn't much but the underwater footage was really good. The stories lacked a lot . . . when I say underwater cowboys, that's really what it was!" Al Hanson was the stand-in for Paul Lukas and Kirk Douglas in *20,000 Leagues Under the Sea*.

Time on the ocean floor sometimes yielded treasure—or trash. Among their many finds was a ship's top lantern, a beautiful 30-inch-tall brass top lantern with its crystal mantel still intact and its lens still in place. Other finds included an antique vase made on a potter's wheel with far-eastern designs, plus cases of anchovies, sardines, wine, dropped pallets of merchan-

BOB PLUNKETT

Norma and Al Hanson performed for the famous glass-bottom boats at Catalina Islands in California. They would walk about the sea floor picking up shells, feeding the fish, and do other activities to the amazed watch of tourists topside.

dise, fillets, and more. On one trip with Norma tending on top, Al sent up a birdcage with a dead bird in it. "This bird isn't even talking to me anymore," he said. Norma said that it was disgusting!

While inspecting the pilings at the bottom of a ship-loading dock, Al found several jugs of wine, apparently lost off a loading ramp during transfer. "The wine was still good, but we don't drink and the clerk and the maintenance people all wanted a jug of wine, so Al sent up some buckets with the wine jugs and we put them in the fish hold which also had the air intake for the compressor," Norma said. As the day wore on and the bottles got warm, they suddenly burst. "With the air intake right there, I suddenly heard Al laughing again, and I got nervous. 'What is it,' I wondered. Turns out the fumes that the compressor pulled from the broken bottles and pumped into his suit made him drunk. He was so drunk when I pulled him up he could hardly walk. Not being a drinking man, a little went a long way. I took his helmet and weights off and he couldn't even stand. 'My gosh,' I thought, 'I didn't want anybody to see him drunk on the job!' " After a few hours on the deck, Al finally woke up feeling very hungry with a terrible hangover. And how about the pilings? "They look just fine," he told her. (Author's interview, 2/26/05; numerous published materials provided by Norma Hanson)

DEVOTION UNDER FIRE

LARGEST INHERITANCE FORFEITED. For the singular but precious purpose of joining the Church in the 1830s, Alfred Bell and his two sisters forfeited their inheritance in the Bell family's sprawling Far Away Hills estate outside of Nashville, Tennessee. A disagreement arose between their father, William Bell, a Revolutionary War veteran and slave owner, and the three of the four children who sought to join the Mormons, who opposed slavery. The Far Away Hills estate that was originally 252 acres still exists to this day and was recently owned by country star Mel Tillis. Today the land appraises for more than $100 million. Alfred Bell was a dedicated friend of the Smiths, and took Joseph and Hyrum Smith across the Mississippi to hide them from the mobs just prior to the martyrdom, and later served as a judge in Lehi, Utah. (Randy Bell, April 18, 2006)

Other courageous Latter-day Saints listed in the master record:
- Don Lind, astronaut
- John Goddard, world-famous explorer
- Richard Jones, oldest man to row solo across the Atlantic
- Sam Cowley, bravest man in the FBI

President Gordon B. Hinckley is the new Mormon World Record holder for being the eldest to ever hold the office of president and prophet of The Church of Jesus Christ of Latter-day Saints. Born June 23, 1910, his birthday in 2007 made him 97 years young. He was ordained the 15th president of the Church on March 12, 1995. On November 2, 2006, he surpassed the longevity record of President David O. McKay, who passed away in 1970 at age 96. President Hinckley passed away on January 27, 2008.

THE CHURCH

MORMON ACHIEVEMENTS BY THE NUMBERS

5—Age of youngest LDS language interpreter
15—Nonstop endowments by an LDS man
15,000—Feet above sea level for highest altitude LDS chapel
1,000,000—Total missionaries dispatched since 1830

WARDS AND BISHOPS

OLDEST BISHOP. Who is the oldest bishop in the Church? In 1999, it was Ralph Arnold Barnes, Carondelet Ward, St. Louis Missouri South Stake. He was called at age 81 years, 8 months, and 23 days on September 17, 1995. Bishop Barnes was released at age 85 years, 10 months, 27 days. (George W. Fuhriman, St. Louis Missouri, 4/6/05)

LONGEST SERVING BRANCH PRESIDENT. In 1968, Max Woodbury, Ogden Utah Branch for the Deaf, Ogden Utah Stake, retired at the oh-so-young age of 91, having served as branch president for 51 years. President Woodbury was the only person to serve in that position until his retirement since the branch was first organized in 1917. Church training for the deaf was started in Salt Lake City in 1892. Five years later, a school for the deaf was organized in Ogden. By 1902, Woodbury became a teacher for the deaf at that school and also agreed to teach them Sunday School. When the first chapel building for deaf Saints was dedicated in 1917, he began his tenure that would exceed half a century. He died at age 96 on December 29, 1973. He and his wife, Kate Forsha,

RAY COCHRAN

Max Woodbury presided over the Ogden Branch for the Deaf for 51 years, helping to lead the way for the establishment of a school for the deaf.

raised two children while serving the deaf for most of their married lives. (Roy Cochran, Roy, Utah; *Ogden Standard Examiner,* 1/13/68, 12/30/77)

FIRST BLACK BISHOP. We're still checking on this one, but right now it appears that Alonzo Harris became the Church's first black bishop over a ward in the Philippines shortly after the 1978 revelation on priesthood and the blacks, given in the late 1970s. He was retired from the Navy and was working as a civilian at Subic Bay Base when he was called. He married a local woman, and they happily served for many years. In the mid-1980s, they moved to Washington state where he served as bishop over the Tacoma 9th Ward, Tacoma Washington North Stake. (George H. Hill III, 5/13/05)

LONGEST STRING OF FAMILY CHURCH LEADERSHIP. Jennifer Hoffman, Gresham Ward, Wausau Wisconsin Stake, reports an amazing string of Church leadership within her family. It all began when Anton and Clara Heins were baptized in 1924 in the Gresham area. When a branch was created in 1936 and Orline H. Maas, a grandson of Anton and Clara, was made branch president, the Heins family legacy began.

1. Orline H. Maas, branch president, 1936–47
2. Everett Maas, branch president, 1947–58 (Anton's grandson)
3. Aubrey O. Stoehr, branch president, 1958–63 (Anton's grandson)
4. Delbert E. Hoffman, branch president, 1963–67 (Anton's grandson)
5. Clyde O. Hoffmann, branch president, 1967–69 (Anton's grandson)
6. Grant A. Stoehr, branch president, 1969–73 (Anton's grandson)
7. Sanford K. Hoffman, branch president, 1973–79 (Anton's grandson)
8. Stephen C. Jensen, branch president, 1979–1984 (married to Anton's great-granddaughter)
9. Daniel D. Hoffman, branch president, 1984–1986 (May 18) (Anton's grandson)
[Branch becomes a ward on May 18, 1986]
10. Daniel D. Hoffmann, bishop, 1986–87 (Anton's grandson)
11. Wayne L. Jeske, bishop, 1987–1992 (Anton's great-grandson)
12. Stephen C. Jenson, bishop, 1992–98 (Same as #8, his second go-round)
13. Jeffrey L. Hoffman, bishop, 1998–2004 (Anton's great-grandson)
14. Patrick D. Pleshek, bishop, 2004–present (married to Anton's great-granddaughter)
(Source: Jennifer Hoffman, 3/29/06)

WHERE THE SAINTS MEET—NORTH AND SOUTH

54° 55' 60 SOUTH LATITUDE: The Puerto Williams Branch is the most southerly branch in the Church. Hanging off the very end of Chile, the small

FILE PHOTO

Puerto Williams is on the southern tip of South America. About 1,800 people live there, most of them working for the Chilean Navy. Pictured here, local members arrive for Sunday services, bundled against the cold.

island community of 1,800 is bounded by Cape Horn and the Strait of Magellan. Ruperto and Leonora Cea de Marquez, converts since the early 1980s, were the first to bring the Church to this remote place in 1987. They've lived there ever since, watching more LDS families and converts build the ranks to almost two dozen. (*Church News,* 8/26/06; photo by Nestor Curbelo)

54° 48' 00 SOUTH LATITUDE: If you're on your way to Antarctica, be sure to stop for church at one of the three branches that meet in two chapels at this most-southern city in the world of Ushuaia, Argentina. And pack your winter coat! (Gerald E. Jones, Harrisville, Utah, 2/11/06)

HIGHEST CHAPEL. The newest Mormon World Record for the highest altitude chapel in the Church is the branch chapel built on the highest plains of the Andes Mountains in Yauri, Espinar, Peru. Part of

BRYAN KUNZ

the Peru Lima Central Mission, Sicuani District, the chapel was dedicated in 2003 and is the nicest structure in that remote Peruvian village. The exact altitude is not known, though the

Elder Bryan J. Kunz took this photo of some local members in front of the highest known LDS chapel in the world, at approximately 15,000 feet above sea level. In comparison, the first base camp to climb Northeast Ridge of Mount Everest is at 17,000 feet.

village is generally considered to be close to 15,000 feet above sea level. The closest documented location is a little lower on the mountain and is listed at 13,460 feet. (Jeffrey K. Kunz and Brian J. Kunz)

AUXILIARY AND OTHER CALLINGS

DELOY AND NADINE ARCHIBALD

102-year-old Charles Adams with his wife, Polly Jane Adams.

OLDEST ELDERS QUORUM PRESIDENT. Charles Adams, newly called elders quorum president in 2006, for the Greensboro Branch, Bessemer Alabama Stake, knew he'd get the support he needed from his wife, Polly Jane Adams, when the call was extended. She always supported him, as a matter of fact, because he was, after all, 102! (*Church News*, 2/25/06)

YOUNG WOMEN

OLDEST LAUREL INSTRUCTOR. If working with the youth keeps you young, then Hilda Leora Durham has mastered that particular fountain of youth. In March 2006, she was called to be the Laurel instructor in the Santa Ana 5th (Spanish) Ward, Santa Ana California South (Spanish) Stake at the young age of 89. "I'm the only English-speaking teacher in the stake," she told the Church News. "But they love me to pieces," she says of her class. (*Church News*, 4/22/06; photo by Sergio Equihaus Sr.)

SERGIO EQUIHAUS SR.

Just one of the girls. Hilda Durham, 89, teaches her Laurel's class in California.

SEMINARY

PERFECT ATTENDANCE—EARLY-MORNING SEMINARY. Who can claim the longest perfect attendance in any particular Church activity? For the Leavitt family of the Lemon Grove Ward, San Diego Sweetwater California Stake, they have a streak that will be tough to match. Sister Shari Leavitt reports that her six oldest children each completed 100% attendance for all four years of early-morning Seminary. (Shari Leavitt, 3/28/06)

ORDINANCES

MOST ENDOWMENT SESSIONS NONSTOP (MALE). On May 16–17, 1997, Mark Baker of the Worcester 1st Ward, Springfield Massachusetts Stake, set a new record for the most endowment sessions nonstop by completing 15 sessions in a 30-hour period. Fortunately for the Baker family, their Stake Temple Day event coincided with a recent program where the Washington, D.C. Temple would remain open Friday night to accommodate stake groups coming from out of town. Brother Baker started at 6 AM Friday morning and just kept going. Between sessions, Brother Baker went to the drinking fountain and had some granola bars stashed in his locker. He finished about noon on the following day with just enough time to board the bus and join the others on the trip back to Massachusetts. "I had a marvelous, spiritual experience as I served . . . for me, I felt like I was home where I belonged, doing the work that I loved." And he slept for most of the 8-hour bus ride home. (Author's interview, 4/10/06)

BAKER FAMILY

Mark and Linley Baker

MOST TEMPLE SEALINGS. So, who keeps track? A lot of grateful married couples, that's who! Brother Ned Winder, Jordan North 2nd Ward, Salt Lake Jordan Utah North Stake, has been a temple sealer since 1978, and according to the Salt Lake Temple Recorder, Brother Winder has married well over 4,000 couples. At the time this record was noted, he was 82 and his phone was constantly ringing as word of mouth spread of this great brother's humor, spirituality, spirit of ease, and joy. He would be the first to say that who performs the ordinance makes no difference for temple marriages, but it is nonetheless, a new Mormon World Record. (Mike Winder, 2/4/05)

WINDER FAMILY

Newlyweds Mike and Karyn Winder with Grandpa Ned behind them. Mike authored the popular *Prophets and Presidents*.

MOST MEN IN A BABY BLESSING CIRCLE. With the Church spreading far and wide, it's hard to contain the most special events to available space, but in 2006, Rob McMaster, Farmington Utah North Stake, reports that for the blessing of his cousin's baby, a giant double circle of priesthood bearers managed to get their hands beneath the new baby, giving the youngster a send off with a total of 35 in the circle. (Rob McMaster, 3/20/06)

YOUNGEST NAME EXTRACTOR. In March 1984, just a week after her eighth birthday, Melanie Minert, Brigham City 18th Ward, Brigham City Utah Stake, became the youngest name extractor in the Church. At the time, her father, Roger F. Minert, was the director of the name extraction program for six stakes in the Brigham City region and had 129 extractors working in seven foreign languages. Melanie extracted names from German church records. (Roger and Jeanne Minert, 11/10/06)

BAPTISM

MOST PROXY BAPTISMS—WOMEN. Who among the sisters of the Church has performed the most proxy baptisms? As of 2005, Wendy Maher from St. Johns, Arizona, had completed 6,002. (Flora M. Ballard, 10/25/05)

GLORIA WRIGHT

Amos R. Wright was in the water almost all day while baptizing 120 Shoshone Indians.

MOST BAPTISMS IN ONE DAY. Amos R. Wright was one of the great early pioneer missionaries who was sent on several missions to the Shoshone Indians. He baptized 87 people in one day. The next morning, others came to the river where Brother Wright was camped so that they too could be baptized. That day he baptized and confirmed another 120. "I was in the water almost constantly until after sundown," he wrote to President John Taylor, "except when confirming and recording." He listed all of the names and pronunciations in a small book that is now in preserved in the Church History Department. Brother Wright also baptized the Shoshone chief and his family. "The Old Man wanted to know how he could be Baptized as he was unable to come up to where the rest came," wrote Brother Wright in his journal. "Accordingly, he sent his young Men and Boys to prepare a place in a Creek Close by, which took them about 2 Hours, they built a log Heap Fire on the Bank, and after the Moon was up so we could see better, I performed the Ordinance for Himself and all his Family 17 Persons, before I left I administered to him." The ill chief was healed and back on his horse the next day. All the temple work was done for these people in the Mesa Arizona Temple. (Gloria Wright, 3/23/05)

UNIQUE BAPTISM. Brother Larry L. Boyd, Cannon 4th Ward, Salt Lake City, writes in to say he was taught the gospel by a Prince and was baptized by a King! (This was Elder Prince and Elder King, of course!). (Larry L. Boyd, 3/3/05)

MOST BAPTISMS BY AN INDIVIDUAL. According to a reference in the *Discourses of President Gordon B. Hinckley*, a good brother named Dan Jones served two missions. He converted 3,600 in his first mission and 2,000 in his second for a total of 5,600. (Gerald E. Jones, Harrisville, Utah, 2/11/06; see *Discourses of President Gordon B. Hinckley*, Vol. 2:369)

FIRST CONVERTS

FIRST BAPTIZED IN KOREA. When the president of South Korea, Syngman Rhee, had an emergency need to speak to his vice-minister of education, he sent his personal secretary to find him. It was a Sunday, and the secretary found the vice-minister teaching Sunday School in his LDS branch. "You'll have to wait until the class is over," Brother Kim Ho Jik said. And the secretary did. When Brother Kim finally arrived at the presidential palace, he was scolded for taking so long, but after explaining his delay, the president patted him on the shoulder and said, "You did well!" Brother Kim was born to Confucian parents and later joined the Presbyterian Church. While studying at Cornell University in New York state, he made friends with Oliver Wayman, a member of the Church. A friendship was formed, the Book of Mormon was delivered, and he was baptized in the Susquehanna River in July 1951. He returned to his country in 1951 when the Korean War was in full blossom. And then in 1955, he escorted President Joseph Fielding Smith and several servicemen to an overlook near Seoul, and there in the quiet peace of privacy, Pres. Smith dedicated the land for missionary work. Brother Kim passed away August 31, 1959, just eight years after his baptism. (Rebecca M. Taylor, *The Friend*, April 1997)

FILE PHOTO

Brother and Sister Kim Ho Jik and their family.

FIRST CONVERTS ABOVE THE ARCTIC CIRCLE. In December of 1906, missionaries visited the Paulsen family in Sommarset, Sweden, and taught them the gospel. The entire family accepted the message and requested baptism. On January 8, 1906, Ingrid Marie Paulsen and some family members were baptized in the Oksfjorden (North Sea) at the small harbor Kalvhupollen on the shores of Hinnöya Island. Due to the frigid temperatures of the water, Ingrid's mother, Karen, who was elderly and frail, wasn't baptized until some time later in the United States. Hinnöya is at 68.64 degrees north latitude. (Ann Heyman, granddaughter of Ingrid Paulsen, 11/7/06)

ANN HEYMAN

A century ago. The Paulsen family was the first to be baptized above the Arctic Circle in 1906. Pictured here, front row (l-r): Unknown child, Edwin Christiansen, Anna Marie Paulsen, unknown child, and Karen Ellingsen Paulsen. Back row (l-r): Paul Paulsen, Ingrid Marie Paulsen, Simon Martin Christiansen, Erling Paulsen, and Abel Paulsen.

FIRST BAPTISM IN JAMAICA. The first convert baptism on the island nation of Jamaica was Paul Schmeil, baptized in a college swimming pool in Mandeville, Jamaica, on December 20, 1970. A handful of LDS families were already living on the island and brought about the conversion work, but these were "transplants" brought by their employers. The Schmeil family became a good foundation for a branch that began to take root in the early 1970s. Within 20 years, the membership had grown to more than 2,000. (Boyd Clark, 2004)

FIRST CONVERT FROM NICARAGUA. Lily Arguello's Uncle Juan Sacasa was the president of Nicaragua in the late 1930s when Somoza overthrew the government. Uncle Sacasa and his family were exiled, and Lily's family moved out as well. They settled in Panama, and Lily hired on as a stewardess with Pan American Airways in 1942. Meanwhile, Robert G. Sorensen was headed home from his mission in Argentina when he waylaid in Panama. Pan Am hired Elder Sorensen for his bilingual capabilities, and that's what set up a budding love story between him and Lily. With both back in the States the following year, he proposed and they were married. After three children, she was baptized on May 4, 1947, and became Lily Arguello Sorensen. (Gigi Berrett, fifth child of Lily and Robert)

GIGI BERRETT

Lily Arguello Sorensen and three of her children. Her uncle was the president of Nicaragua who was overthrown by Somoza, putting her on a path to meet the gospel and her husband.

OTHER "FIRST CONVERTS" listed in the master record (if you know of a correction or addition to this list, please contact the author at www.mormonworldrecords.com):

> **Above the Arctic Circle:** Pete Davis (1959, now surpassed by Ingrid Marie Paulsen in 1906; see her write-up on previous page)
> **Bolivia:** Maria Van Gemeron
> **Corsica:** Ginetter Caillard
> **Malaysia:** Peter Chandran
> **Cambodia:** Francis Cheung King Shaang
> **Russia:** Johan M. Lindlof
> **Thailand:** Srilaksana Gottsche
> **Siberia:** Andrew Hasberg
> **England:** George Darling Watt
> **Chile:** Ricardo Garcia Orellrana
> **Spain:** Jose Olivera
> **Kosrae:** Isidro Abraham
> **Newfoundland:** Lavinia Webber Mercer
> **Bangladesh:** Towhit-Ul-Alam

GENEALOGY

LARGEST FREE ONLINE GENEALOGY SITES. FamilySearch.org, the Church's online genealogy search system, has grown to be the largest free service in the world. Here's how the system has grown, as of 2007:

- **Launch date:** May 24, 1999
- **Number of names in searchable databases:** over 1 billion
- **Number of hits since launch:** over 15 billion
- **Number of visitors since launch:** over 150 million
- **Number of pages viewed since launch:** over 5 billion
- **Number of hits per day:** over 10 million
- **Number of visitors per day:** over 50,000
- **Number of pages viewed per day:** over 1 million
- **Number of registered users:** over 1 million
- **Number of collaboration e-mail lists:** over 200,000

(Source: www.familysearch.org)

GENERAL CONFERENCE

TEN MOST MEMORABLE GENERAL CONFERENCES. Here's a list of firsts and achievements that will change and evolve over time as the Church grows and expands. As of this writing, here are the top 10 most memorable Conferences (thanks to Davis Bitton for compiling this):

- October 1844—first conference after the assassination of the Prophet Joseph Smith.
- October 1848—Brigham Young was unanimously sustained as president of the Church.
- October 1867—The first conference in the new Salt Lake Tabernacle was held.
- April 1877—Conference was held in the "fully dedicated" St. George Temple, and Brigham Young announced an extensive reorganization of stakes.
- April 1919—No conference because of the influenza epidemic.
- April 1930—Centennial celebration. B. H. Roberts presented his six-volume *Comprehensive History of the Church*.
- April 1936—In the depths of the Depression, President Heber J. Grant announced the Church's welfare program.
- April 1942—With the war imposing rationing on gasoline, conference was limited to 500 leaders in the Assembly Hall, a practice that continued until 1945.
- April 1951—David O. McKay sustained as Church president, and J. Reuben Clark moved from first to second counselor. Responding to

rumors of a demotion, President Clark said, "In the service of the Lord, it is not where you serve but how."

- October 2001—Following the 9/11 terror attacks in America, President Gordon B. Hinckley assured the Saints that the calamity of times was not yet upon us, but we should continue to be faithful in our preparations for self sufficiency—not in panic, but in wisdom.

FIRST TO INCLUDE A SPORTS SCORE. Though nobody would openly admit it, many of those attending the priesthood session of conference in October 1983 had to be torn away from a great BYU–UCLA football game that Saturday evening. President Gordon B. Hinckley was generous in his sympathies to the football fans and, toward the end of the meeting, announced over the pulpit that BYU had upset UCLA 37–35. It may have been the first sports score announced during general conference and may be the first in the Salt Lake Tabernacle. Some old-timers report they remember President David O. McKay giving a baseball score during conference. Can anyone provide the details?

MISSIONARY WORK

MISSIONARY ENDURANCE EVENTS! Many of us have had them, those variety of challenges while "out in the field" that we thought would never go away, and then later we look back upon with fondness and gratitude. Did you have any such experiences?

- **Longest in One City.** Julio Arciniega reports that upon arriving in the Mexico Torreon Mission, he was sent to the city of Ciudad Juarez for a straight 20 months. The last four months of his mission were in the Mission Home as mission secretary. (Julio Arciniega, 11/10/04)
- **Longest Companionship.** Not only did Elder Arciniega (see above) have the longest stay in one city during these modern times of frequent transfers, but for half of that time he was paired with that very elder with whom he had the most difficult time of all trying to get along! For 10 months, he endured. And he was that other elder's *only* junior companion! (Julio Arciniega, 11/10/04)

MISSION GEOGRAPHY, SMALLEST AND LARGEST

The smallest LDS Church mission in terms of square footage is the Utah Salt Lake Temple Square Mission, where single sister missionaries and older couple

FILE PHOTO

Temple Square: smallest mission in the Church.

missionaries from around the world provide tour-guide services around Temple Square. Many of these far-traveled missionaries find themselves perfectly positioned to serve as hosts to people from their own homelands. A "tour of duty" at Temple Square typically lasts for six months, and then they are reassigned to another mission in the U.S. for another six months, and their last six months is back at Temple Square.

The largest LDS Church mission, geographically, is the Micronesia Guam Mission. Its boundaries enclose an area about the same size as the continental United States, although most of that is empty ocean. The largest mission on land, which also happens to have the most people of any LDS mission, is the China Hong Kong Mission. This mission covers almost all of the Chinese landmass and its population. However, the missionaries serving there are restricted to working in Hong Kong and Macau only. (Church Almanac)

YOUNGEST MISSIONARY COUPLE. Eugene and Charlotte England served at the age of 21 in American Samoa as a full-time missionary couple. They moved to Hawaii a year or so later so Sister England could have her baby born there. Brother England later authored a book, *Making Peace*, in which he dealt with some challenging questions. (Gerald E. Jones, Harrisville, Utah, 2/11/06)

MOST MISSION PRESIDENTS IN ONE FAMILY. In 1975, Richard Oscarson was called to be mission president of the Sweden Stockholm Mission. The following July 26, 1976, his brother Paul was called as president over the new Sweden Goteborg Mission. And then their father, Roy W. Oscarson, was called as mission president over a new mission headquartered in Glasgow, Scotland. (*Church News*, 1/17/98)

LONGEST RUNNING MISSION REUNION. Can anybody beat 70+ years? In 1937, Elder John W. Boud met with fellow missionaries in a London hotel just before he returned home. They formed The Windsor Group and have been meeting monthly for decades and only recently changed the meeting to twice yearly. Among its surviving members was Gordon B. Hinckley! (Thomas J. Boud, 1/12/05)

MOST MISSIONARIES FROM ONE FAMILY. This is a challenging record to call because the definition of "one family" can get complicated. So, submissions are invited!

16: The Leigh R. and Fern Evans family of the Cottonwood 7th Ward, Salt Lake Big Cottonwood Stake:

Gary—Spain Barcelona
Linda Kay—Washington Spokane
Clark—Argentina Cordoba
Mark—Philippines Baguio
Stephen—California San Bernardino
Bruce—Chile/Osorno Vina del Mar
Sally Ann—Montana Billings
John—California San Bernardino, Riverside

(*Church News*, 9/22/07; photo-Evans family)

EVANS FAMILY

The Leigh R. and Fern Evans family

14: The John W. And Sharon R. Boud family of Salt Lake City sent 12 sons, and besides serving missions themselves, they were also serving as mission President in Pennsylvania:.

John W. and Sharon R. Boud—
    British Isles, Northern States
    respectively
John W. Boud, Jr.—Austria
David C. Boud—Wisconsin
James R. Boud—England
Joseph R. Boud—Japan
Stephen R. Boud—Germany

14: The A. Lee and Carol Ann Bahr family of the Mueller Park 9th Ward, Bountiful Utah Mueller Park Stake:

Erick Bahr—Denver South
Mary Lynn—Washington DC

Robby—Canada Winnipeg
Kathy—Argentina Buenos Aires North
Jeremy—Ecuador Quayaquil
Cameron—New York New York
Micah—Costa Rica San Hose
Brooks—Mexico Hermosillo

BAHR FAMILY

The A. Lee and Carol Ann Bahr family

ODDS AND ENDS

BUNNY STONE

Bunny Melendez (Stone) translates for Elder Hugh B. Brown.

Youngest Language Interpreter. On March 8, 1965, five-year-old Bunny Melendez was attending the Colegio A. D. Palmer LDS school in Santiago, Chile, when Elder Hugh B. Brown came by for a visit. An interpreter was needed, so the school's director, Dale Harding, scooped up Bunny in his arms and she translated Elder Brown's comments into Spanish, and questions and comments made back into English. Today Bunny (Melenez) Stone and her family make their home in the Timpanogos Park 4th Ward, Orem Utah North Stake. (Author's interview, 4/9/05)

MOST ACTIVE VOLUNTEER STATE. At the end of a three-year study by the federally funded Corporation for National and Community Service, Utah stood above all other states with a volunteer rate of 43.5 percent for

2006, far ahead of the national average of 26.7 percent. That same year, 790,000 volunteers in Utah donated 145.8 million hours of service. The survey showed that Utah is only one of five states where teaching or tutoring is the most popular volunteer activity. It also showed that 73 percent of those who volunteered in 2005 also volunteered in 2006, meaning Utah is the sixth highest state for volunteer retention. It also ranked first for the highest volunteer rate in the nation for young adults, college students, and older adults. Utah took second place behind Nebraska for volunteer baby boomers. (*Church News*, 5/5/07)

PAUL B. SKOUSEN

The Frisbee is one of the greatest entertainment toys ever invented, with more than 200,000,000 brand-name Frisbees produced worldwide, and untold millions more of various copycat versions. The inventor of this amazing flying disk is Walter Frederick Morrison, 87, of Richfield, Utah, whose pioneer roots run as deep as any in the central valleys of Utah. Shown in this 2007 photo with Kathy B. Skousen, Fred has just given her an autographed replica of his original Pluto Platter.

KNOWLEDGE

MORMON ACHIEVEMENTS BY THE NUMBERS

10—Years BYU ranked number one as stone-cold sober college in America

1,670—Years old for the world's oldest pine that also lives in Utah

273,600—Highest price in dollars paid for an original LDS hymnal

200,000,000—Frisbees sold since their invention by a Mormon

THINKERS

DISASTER EXPERT. Dubbed by the media as the "Master of Disaster," Randall Bell, Rancho Santa Margarita Ward, California, is an applied economist and widely regarded as the world's top authority on measuring the economic impacts of disasters. He consulted on the World Trade Center site, the Flight 93 crash site, the North Ridge Earthquake, the LA Riots, the Bikini Atoll Nuclear Test sites, as well as the Jon Benet Ramsey, Heaven's Gate, and OJ Simpson crime scenes. Randall's career has been profiled by *People* magazine, The Associated Press, the *Wall Street Journal*, and every major television network. Randall wrote the textbook *Real Estate Damages* and various valuation methodologies that he authored that were later incorporated into federal guidelines for property valuation. (Orell Anderson, MAI, Laguna Beach, CA, 4/18/06)

FIRST NATIONAL SCIENCE FAIR WINNER. Wayne B. Young, a senior at Provo High in Provo, Utah, and a member of the Oak Hills 4th Ward, Edgemont Utah Stake, took first place in the pharmaceutical division of the National Science Fair-International held in Kansas City, Missouri, May 10–13, 1961. He had qualified for the nationals by winning the Utah Science Fair earlier that school year with his exploration into the

WAYNE B. YOUNG

Exploring the potential of antibiotics in mushrooms won Wayne B. Young (right) the National Science Fair Award in 1961.

antibiotic properties of mushrooms. He grew mushrooms in the laboratory at Provo High and used the facilities at BYU and Utah Valley Hospital to create cultures. He injected varying doses of the cultures into animals. They suffered no ill effects as would have been expected from eating raw toadstools. The promise of an antibiotic from mushrooms remained for others to explore, but for Brother Young, it was a new Mormon World Record. Today, Brother Young is a practicing dentist in Utah County. (Author's interview, 2005)

SPELLING BEE FINALISTS. Tia Natasha-Elizabeth Thomas, 12, of the Oakhurst Ward, Fresno California West Stake, tied for eighth place in the 2007 Scripps National Spelling Bee Championship in Washington, D.C. on May 31, 2007. Tia was homeschooled and successfully spelled such monster words as *periostracum*, *syssarocis*, *impercipient*, and *bewusstseinslage*. She was ousted on *zacate*. This was Tia's fourth consecutive trip to the national, a record only two other 12-year-olds in the country share with her. One other has gone five years straight. (*Church News*, 6/9/07)

NATIONAL MATH CHAMPION, U.S. It's a grueling exercise for those of us not mathematically inclined, but each year there's a contest held to find the best team and individual mathematicians across the country. Sponsored by the American Region Mathematics League (ARML), more than 100 teams of 1,800 students compete to see who knows their "stuff" the best. On June 3, 2006, Samuel Dittmer, 16, of the Zionsville Ward, Indianapolis Indiana North Stake, not only helped his team win their site contest (at the University of Iowa), but he went on to win the National Individual Championship. For the Individual competition, each student was given four pairs of problems and 10 minutes each to solve them. Samuel was the only person to get all eight correct. How would you fare with these from his actual test?

I–1. Compute the number of positive integers that have the same number of digits when expressed in base 3 and base 5.

I–2. Two 3 by 4 rectangles overlap in such a way that their sides are perpendicular. If the area and perimeter of the shaded region are 22 and 20 respectively, compute AB.

I–3. If $ABCDE$ is a regular pentagon and $MNCD$ is a square, compute the value of $m\angle AMN - m\angle EAM$ in degrees.

I–4. Compute the four-digit positive integer N whose square root is three times the sum of the digits of N.

I–5. Starting with $n = 1$, let $\{a_n\}$ be an infinite geometric sequence with $a_2 = 17$. Compute the smallest possible positive sum of the sequence.

I–6. Determine the sum of the y-coordinates of the four points of intersection of $y = x^4 - 5x^2 - x + 4$ and $y = x^2 - 3x$.

I–7. If $\log_8 a + \log_8 b = (\log_8 a)(\log_8 b)$ and $\log_a b = 3$, compute the value of a.

I–8. There are 5 computers, A, B, C, D, and E. For each pair of computers a coin is flipped. If it is heads, then a link is built between the two computers; if it is tails, there's no link between the two. Every message that a computer receives is sent to every computer to which it is linked. Compute the probability that every computer is able to receive messages from every other computer.

(*Church News*, 9/30/06; http://www.arml.com)

MOST LICENSES, ENGINEERING. When John Reese Leavitt, Melba 2nd Ward, Kuna Idaho Stake, earned his civil engineering degree at BYU in 1978, he had no idea his employment would lead him to become licensed in all 50 states, all U.S. territories, several Canadian provinces, the Philippines, and Indonesia. With more than 70 engineering licenses, he can practice his trade just about anywhere English is spoken. But perhaps his greatest claim to fame is his World Famous Manually Self-Operated Butt-Kicking Machine. Brother Leavitt invented the device to celebrate his engineering firm's 10th

LEAVITT ENGINEERING

The Manually Self-Operated Butt-Kicking Machine swings a tennis shoe or boot of choice from beneath into a hole in the seat for the appropriate surprise reminder—or punishment!

year anniversary. The victim sits in an oddly shaped chair, pulls a lever, and a bright red Converse shoe pops through a hole and hits the person square in the tush. News of the invention was covered by international press! (Hollie Leavitt, 11/12/04)

EXECUTIVES

WWW. DELL.COM

Kevin B. Rollins

DELL COMPUTERS. Kevin B. Rollins, Round Rock, Texas, succeeded Dell Computers' founder, Michael S. Dell, in July 2004 and took over the operations of the world's largest mail-order computer giant. One of the problems he found was that the corporate culture at Dell had been soured by greed. He instituted a program where underlings would evaluate their bosses. He was surprised to get feedback on his own weaknesses. Some said he was so icy cold that his personality should be stored in a meat locker. But the feedback program is still in place at Dell, and seems to have helped with the attitudes. He resigned in 2007 to pursue other opportunities. Personally, he is an accomplished violinist, sometimes performing publicly, but also skis, mountain bikes, and races motorcycles and cars. He and his wife, Debra (Skinner), are the parents of four children. (*Deseret News,* 9/13/05)

INVENTIONS

FILE PHOTOS

Top: Pem Farnsworth in 1927, the first televised face in history. Bottom: Pem toward the end of her life.

FIRST TELEVISED FACE. The LDS inventor of the television, Philo Farnsworth, met his bride, Elma "Pem" Garner, in 1923. They were married May 27, 1926, and later sealed in the Salt Lake Temple. When Philo completed his invention of the very first working electronic television, he invited the help of Pem and her brother Cliff for tests in San Francisco in 1927. After proving the new technology by transmitting the brief movement of an etched line on a piece of glass, they tried to see how a human would appear. Pem's was the first televised face in human history. Under the glaring heat of many lights, experiments were conducted to improve the quality of the image, and Sister Farnsworth patiently waited while history was made. She passed away April 27, 2006. (*Deseret News,* 5/7/06)

DIGITAL SOUND. In the early 1970s Robert B. Ingebretsen, Salt Lake City, partnered with Dr. Tomas Stockham of the University of Utah physics department to pioneer the development of digital sound. Brother Ingebretsen received an Oscar in 1999 for his work. As a masters degree project at the University of Utah, he developed a way of sampling music at 30,000 times a second and storing the information on a computer. Unraveling all of that information required a special decoder. This process gave birth to the digital world we know today. Next time you play a music CD, remember that you're using Brother Ingebretson's decoder idea! He also created the world's first digital movie with the help of Brother Ed Catmull. The movie was a 20-second portrait of a human hand. Brother Ingebretsen's ultimate gift to the world was historical in every sense of the word: CDs, DVDs, digital music, and movies! He passed away on March 3, 2003, at age 54. (Ivan Dyreng, 12/28/04)

FRISBEE. The amazing flying disk that today is known worldwide as the Frisbee made its debut in the late 1940s. Walter Frederick Morrison, 87, of Richfield, Utah, fondly remembers tossing around pie tins, cake pans, paint-can lids, and popcorn lids as a boy before thinking such a flying disk could be perfected and marketed. After World War II, the whole UFO craze started after rumors of an alien

F. MORRISON

Fred Morrison

space craft crashing near Roswell, New Mexico. Brother Morrison and his buddies became so adept at flying the variously shaped disks that he actually made some money by selling them. A cake pan that worked the best was bought by somebody for $.25, and with hamburgers costing $.19, he and his buddy only had to sell two to get lunch! But that started him on how he could design an improved flying disk to catch the UFO craze, and he started working on a prototype. By 1948, he had saved enough to get a mold made and started mass production. His creation would be known as Flyin-Saucers. In 1951 he was calling them Pluto Platters, and that's when the co-founders of Wham-O came along.

An original Frisbie's Pies pan

They bought the marketing rights in January 1957, and six months later they changed the name. "Frisbie" was a nickname for flying disks that came from the empty pie tins college boys used to throw around from the now-defunct Connecticut bakery, the Frisbie Pie Co. When Wham-O co-founder Rich Knerr decided to change the name Brother Morrison had been using to the traditional name Frisbie, he wasn't

FRED MORRISON

PAUL B. SKOUSEN

Re-issued classic Frisbee: autographed for posterity.

sure how to spell the word and accidently coined a new word, Frisbee. Its popularity took off like a rocket with sales today in excess of 200 million, not to mention the sales of more than 60 other manufacturers of flying discs. Frisbee golf sporting events now dot the planet, as do other Frisbee activities of tag or with dogs or just backyard throwing. In 1968, the U.S. Navy spent $400,000 in a study of Frisbees for use as a flare launcher. Meanwhile, Brother Morrison has retired from his job as a building inspector in California, and makes his home in Richfield, Utah. (Interview with Walter Fred Morrison, 7/4/07; *Richfield Reaper,* 3/28/06; About. com; *Deseret News,* 5/15/04)

FIRST TO USE THE BABY JOGGER. Working at a firm in the mid-1970s in Chicago left Brent Ayre little time to see his two- and three-year-old children. Being a devoted father as well as an avid long-distance runner inspired Brent with the idea to push his children in an umbrella stroller as he ran. Before long, he ran with them in long-distance races, immediately catching the attention of media. Thinking this might catch on, Brent sent a video of him that had recently been aired by a large network to the largest manufacturers of baby strollers. (Brent Ayre, 2/10/06)

HOME FITNESS MACHINE. In 2005, BYU engineers built the prototype of a home fitness machine called the Y-Flex. It has two rows of bendable fiberglass poles with guides, and the user feels the same sense of resistance as what free weights offer. Professors Larry Howell and Spencer Magleby developed the machine to transfer motion and energy without using movable parts. (*Church News,* 2/26/05; photo by BYU)

BYU NEWSNET

BYU's Y-Flex fitness machine

RODEO CHUTE. The first known rodeo chute was designed and built by rodeo producer Ray Knight, Payson, Utah. He immigrated to Alberta, Canada, in 1899 to manage his father's million-acre ranch. In 1902, just one year after the town Raymond (named after Ray Knight) was founded on the Knight Ranch, he produced Canada's first rodeo, the Raymond Stampede. He became the world's richest and largest rodeo stock producer with 18,000 head of cattle and 2,000 head of horses for use in his rodeo shows. He financed the building of the first rodeo arena in Canada with a covered grandstand and an engineered race track. He introduced his newly invented rodeo chute in 1903. (John Bascom, 9/10/06)

BYU FACTS AND FEATS

STONE-COLD SOBER. It's an admirable honor in the eternal scheme of things, but widely mocked among those in the great and spacious buildings that dot this fair land. What is this mighty feat that draws praise and scorn? It's BYU and an honor code that has led young adults through the best years of their lives unscathed by the vices and nonsense that plague their peers from coast to coast. In 2007, BYU racked up its 10th consecutive ranking as the number one "stone-cold sober" school in *Princeton Review*'s annual review of colleges. The *Review* queries 115,000 students from 361 U.S. colleges regard-

SECRET CAT SCAN

No drunk Cougars at BYU, although a few stray cats have indulged in a wee too much hair of the dog.

ing their school's campus life, student body, and academics. Trailing BYU's example were the U.S. Coast Guard, Air Force, and Navy academies for the fewest students imbibing in a little hair of the dog!

Other BYU Rankings:
#1—Students pray on a regular basis
#1—Least hard liquor consumed
#1—Least beer consumed
#1—Future Rotarians and Daughters of the American Revolution (most traditional valued)
#2—Least use of marijuana
#3—Best college library
#4—Most nostalgic for Ronald Reagan (Conservative)

(www.cnn 8/20/07, citing the *Princeton Review*)

MOST PHYSICS TEACHERS GRADUATED. In a day when technology rules, America's physical sciences and engineering edge is eroding. Leading institutions and think tanks point to a lack of preparedness. Recent statistics show that nationwide the greatest shortage of teachers is for special education, followed by English as a second language, and coming in a strong third is a need for physics teachers. In 2006, BYU graduated 16 physics teachers, the most of any school and many states' schools combined. This represented 5 percent of the country's total. At BYU, physics majors are reminded that they can also get a teaching certificate. The pay is far less, averaging about $33,000. But a strong plus for BYU's physics graduates is that many of them are returned missionaries and have learned to love teaching, and that has carried over into many of the graduates now moving out across the country to keep America's technological prowess moving upward. (*Daily Herald*, 6/11/07; *Deseret News*, 6/18/07)

FIRST EVOLUTION CLASS AT BYU. The debate over organic evolution reaches back a century when early Church brethren and LDS scientists grappled with theories and evidences. Nothing came of it "back in the day," and the Church at that time (1909) took no official position on evolution other than to say man was created in God's image and the earth was created by Him, with no declaration of the processes involved. For several decades, the subject was taboo until 1956 when Dr. Howard Stutz was allowed to teach a class without using the word *evolution*. Instead, it was called *speciation*. In 1958, he was allowed to change the class name to Organic Evolution. The subject has been taught at BYU ever since. (Ellen Landeen, Howard Stutz, 3/28/06)

LIVING WORLD

GEORGE AND MIMI MURDOCK

Father of migratory beekeeping: Nephi Ephriam Miller, 1873–1940

BEE KEEPING—WORLD'S FIRST MIGRATORY BEEKEEPING. Leave it to members of the Church to invent a way to maximize honey production in the land flowing with milk and honey. In 1894 a young 20-year-old, Nephi Miller, was in Cache Valley, Utah, watching in amazement as his friends worked their colonies of honeybees. Nephi put on the bee veil and gloves and tried it himself. To his amazement, he wasn't afraid of the bees and they were not afraid of him. He asked his father, Jacob Miller, if he could trade five bags of leftover oats for seven bee colonies that were owned by the neighbor, and promised to tend the bees without skipping any of his other duties on the family farm. Dad agreed, and Nephi began building up a business.

After a couple of years of selling honey to his neighbors, Nephi expanded and started selling honey to local merchants. This worked well for a while, and then something amazing took place. In December 1907 Nephi made a trip to California to secure ideas and equipment to render beeswax. Beeswax was a by-product from honey farming that was also a profitable business.

GEORGE AND MIMI MURDOCK

Flying south for the winter. Using trucks and trains, Nephi Miller was the first to maximize honey production by moving millions of bees from snowy Utah to warmer California climates during the cold seasons.

While Nephi traveled around the San Bernardino and Riverside areas, he observed honeybees everywhere very busy at work—in December no less! While back in Utah, his bees were all hibernating and by spring, many of his bees would be dead from the cold—a typical but costly loss each year.

And then the idea hit him. Why not send his bees to California in the winter months and return them in the spring? It could work, he decided, and he lined up transportation contracts with the railroad and trucks. Nephi began moving bee colonies from cold climates to warm climates, and thereby created the world's first commercial migratory bee business.

GEORGE AND MIMI MURDOCK

Nephi Miller, standing at the far left, working with a crew tending to a million bees.

GEORGE AND MIMI MURDOCK

Rita Skousen Miller had her own specialty brand of honey that is still available today called Rita Miller's Clover. A few years back she turned the company over to her daughter Mimi and husband George Murdock of Orem, Utah, who have helped build the business into a highly respected worldwide sweet success story.

By the 1930s, he was moving more than 5 million bees each season, and the golden sweetness was flowing by the ton under the Miller's label. By the 1940s, Miller's Honey had grown into the largest honey manufacturing and distribution company in North America, surpassing production of 180 million pounds in 1941. At its peak, the company managed more than 40,000 colonies in the western United States. Of note were the specialty honey packs that became popular, especially Rita Miller's Clover that is still packed in glass containers and sold nationwide today. Miller's Honey remains a respected international honey distributor and broker, working honey deals across North America and with dozens of countries worldwide, every year. (Rita Skousen Miller, *Sweet Journey*, 1994; George and Mimi Miller Murdock, 2007)

LARGEST PUMPKIN. The largest pumpkin grown by a Latter-day Saint weighed in at 1,104 pounds at the Utah Giant Pumpkin Growers 2006 Weigh-Off on October 8, 2006. Kenny Blair, Bountiful, Utah, also became the first to grow a pumpkin in Utah that exceeded 1,000 pounds. "I think I got some really good seed," he told the *Deseret Morning News*. Giant pumpkin seed has its own genealogy and is named after the grower and the champion pumpkin's weight. Brother Blair's pumpkin seed will be sold to other pumpkin-growing hopefuls as "1104 Blair." To grow a giant pumpkin, Blair prepares the soil in the fall with high ni-

trogen fertilizer and sulfur, adding urea and humate in the spring, plus a spray of cattle-grade backstairs molasses. Horse manure helps, but not too much. After the plants start, he fertilizes with seaweed and fish emulsion, and several pesticides and fungicides, and when a good pumpkin sets, he prunes to leave just one on each plant. As for water, he lets misting sprinklers water the plant two to three minutes every

KENNY BLAIR

The new Mormon World Record champion pumpkin was grown by Kenny Blair in 2006, weighing in at 1,104 pounds.

PAUL B. SKOUSEN

Gordon Tanner of Kaysville, Utah, grew this giant in 2005, setting the 2005 Mormon World Record at 932.5 pounds. He beat his own best the following year with a 963.5-pounder.

40 minutes—this helps them gain 10–15 pounds a day. He buries the vines so they will root after pruning it to maximize output. As the pumpkins grow, he applies calcium baths and soaks towels in Yield Booster and water, and drapes them over the pumpkins every couple of days. All of that and a tarp and propane lantern to ward off early frost, and you too can try growing a giant pumpkin! "We measured some leaves," he said, "and some are 52 inches in diameter. Nobody can believe how big the leaves are!"

In 2006, the Gordon Tanner family of the Windridge Ward, Kaysville Utah Haight Creek Stake, produced a 963.5-pound pumpkin, a new personal best. He held the Mormon World Record for largest pumpkins in 2004 (906 pounds) and 2005 (932.5 pounds). (Author's interview, 12/10/04)

FIVE?! EWE'VE GOT TO BE KIDDING! Among any large mammal breed, quintuplets are a rarity. But Richard Anderson of Wellsville, Utah, didn't know how very uncommon this was until news began to spread about his sheep giving birth to five lambs. March 24, 2005, marks the day when Anderson had left a mother sheep and her two new lambs one evening only to return in the morning to find an additional three lambs. American sheep reproduce at a rate of 1.01 lambs annually per ewe, making this quintuplet event quite unusual. Mother sheep are only outfitted for feeding two at a time, which added up to many midnight bottle feedings by Anderson. (*Herald Journal*, 03/28/05;)

FILE PHOTO

Lamb chops came in fives for Richard Anderson in 2005.

PENGUIN PAMPERING. In 2006, some LDS women from the coastal town of Coffs Harbour, New Zealand, lent their knitting expertise to help the local fairy penguins with form-fitting wool sweaters. The problem they were fighting is the aftermath of oil spills off the coast of Australia. These foot-tall penguins are often caught in the slimy mess that can destroy their natural oils and lead to their deaths. The doll-sized sweaters are given to rescued penguins to keep them warm and stop the preening and ingesting of poisonous oil while a new layer of protective feathers can grow. Sisters Jenny Allen and Marion Braun heard about the problems the penguins were having and organized about 800 knitters aged 50 to 80 to produce more than 1,800 sweaters. The colorful sweaters are now part of the tourism as visitors stop by to see the penguins parade around in their assorted and colorful regalia. Local souvenir stores have a brisk business of selling surplus sweaters on toy penguins. (*Salt Lake Tribune*, 4/19/06)

LDS CHURCH

Sweaters protect penguins caught in oil spills until the critter's feathers grow back.

MATTHEW BEKKER

OLDEST LIMBER PINE TREE (2007). An ancient, gnarly old tree near the Alta ski resort in Utah has been dubbed "Twister," for its massive trunk that stretches almost barkless to more than 50 feet tall. At 1,704 years old, as of 2007, it is the oldest such tree in the world. Data collected from the tree will help scientists extract climate data along the Wasatch Front to about AD 303. (*BYU Magazine*, Spring 2007)

The world's largest and oldest limber pines live in Utah.

BIGGEST LIMBER PINE TREE (1996). The largest limber pine in the world measures in on a ridge south of Snowbird, Utah. It measures 56 feet high, 87.4 inches around the trunk, with a crown that spreads 46 feet.

JUDICIAL

FILE PHOTO

George Sutherland

SUPREME COURT. The closest we can come to having a Latter-day Saint serving as a justice on the U.S. Supreme Court is George Sutherland. He was born to British parents on March 25, 1862. The same year, the family joined the Church and immigrated to Springville, Utah. George's father renounced his faith after a while, and George grew up as a non-Mormon. In 1879, he enrolled at the Brigham Young Academy in Provo and became a friend of Karl G. Maeser. After law school in Michigan, he returned to Utah and joined the Liberal Party with the goal of ending polygamy. After polygamy was voluntarily abolished, he switched parties and helped organize the GOP in Utah. He won election as Utah's congressman and returned to Washington as Utah's U.S. senator. President Warren G. Harding appointed Sutherland to fill a vacancy on the Supreme Court. He was strongly opposed to government control over private rights, and when Franklin D. Roosevelt tried to push through his New Deal legislation, Sutherland won a reputation as one of the "nine old men of the court" who stood in the way of Roosevelt's socializing of America and stopped his attempt to pack the Supreme Court with New Deal supporters. (John Bascom, *Utah History to Go*)

HIGHEST LDS JUDGE, U.S. In 2005, Thomas B. Griffith, former stake president at BYU, now residing in McLean, Virginia, won confirmation to the U.S. Court of Appeals for the D.C. Circuit. The Senate sustained his nomination by a vote of 73–24. "It's not comfortable to be part of a process where some people are saying unkind things about you," Brother Griffith told the *Deseret Morning News*. In typical Washington locked-horn fashion, some senators picked apart his qualifications because he forgot to pay his bar association dues in the late 1990s. He paid them a few days later and everything was reinstated. Griffith was in the crosshairs of some senators because he was the U.S. Senate's lead counsel during President Clinton's impeachment. (*Deseret News*, 3/14/06)

FILE PHOTO

Thomas B. Griffith, U.S. Court of Appeals for the D.C. circuit

SCIENCE / ENGINEERING

HIGHEST AMUSEMENT RIDE (2004 WORLD RECORD). In 1996, Brother Stan Checketts of Logan, Utah, installed his latest thrill ride sensation, the Big Shot atop the Stratosphere Tower in Las Vegas. The Big Shot uses compressed air to launch 16 passengers at an almost instant 45 miles per hour up a 160-foot tower, rising from a platform 921 feet off the ground and topping out at 1,081 feet, and then gently bouncing the riders back to the starting position. Like an astronaut, riders feel four Gs on the way up and negative Gs on the way down as legs, arms, and hair dangle in the Las Vegas skyline. Brother Checketts and his wife, Sandy, started SandS Worldwide

WWW.S-POWER.COM

The Big Shot in Las Vegas.

Inc. in 1994—today, it's the largest manufacture of amusement park rides in America. Their company has installed more than 150 major amusement rides and coasters and 180 additional children's rides in 27 countries, providing thrills of a lifetime to tens of millions of joy riders. Their creations have been featured in *Forbes, Reader's Digest, The Rolling Stone,* and just about everywhere else. (Stan Checketts, 11/12/04)

Stan Checketts builds the most amazing amusement rides in the world.

WWW.S-POWER.COM

BIGGEST OBSERVATION TOWER IN THE U.S. Before Brother Stan Checketts could put an entertainment ride on top of the Stratosphere, it was engineer Brent Wright, a bishop of a Las Vegas ward, who had to design it. Brother Wright was the sole engineer of the Stratosphere in Las Vegas. In 1996, it was the biggest observation tower in America and the tallest free-standing tower west of the Mississippi. It was completed in 1996 and stands 1,149 feet high. Its solid cement footing is 50 feet thick. (John Bascom, 5/7/06)

WWW.S-POWER.COM

Fastest in the world! Stan Checketts's masterpiece takes you from 0 to 100 mph in under 2 seconds.

FASTEST ROLLER COASTER (2002 WORLD RECORD). The world's fastest roller coaster was designed and built by Stan Checketts, Logan, Utah, and his company for the recreation park Fujikyu Highlands in Japan. Dubbed "Dodompa," this compressed air-launched creation accelerates from 0 to 100 miles per hour in under two seconds. Its fastest speed set the new world record of 107 mph . . . and passengers lived to tell about it (after they calmed down!). (Stan Checketts, 11/12/04)

LONGEST PLAYING TIME ON ATARI. Shawn Davies, member of the Millcreek 9th Ward, Salt Lake Millcreek Stake, got more than stiff knee joints at the arcade T's-N-Tilts on July 23, 1980. He set a world record for the longest time of play at 28 hours and 32 minutes straight with only brief five-minute breaks playing on Atari's Asteroids game while at the same time shattering the previous record of 7,200,000 points with his own 14,000,000. This self-determination began when the arcade owner asked him several months earlier to see how long he could play on one quarter. Fourteen hours and 10,000,000 points later, he stopped, although he determined to come back better prepared and have another go once he heard his record had been broken. Both events were acknowledged by Atari, *TV Guide*, and *Reader's Digest*, as well as local newspapers and news stations. (Shawn Davies, 11/18/04)

FILE PHOTO

Shawn Davies smashed the old world record for Asteroids with almost double the points after a 28-hour marathon.

FIRST LDS VIDEO GAME. Introduced in 2004, Outpost Zarahemla is a lot of fun to play, according to those who have reviewed it. Developed by Wahoo Studios, the game pits Elder Hero against the vicissitudes of frequent visitors to the outpost space station to which he and his trainer are assigned. There is plenty of humor throughout, and though written for teens, it has been popular for all ages. (*Daily Universe*, 9/23/04)

FILE PHOTO

Outpost Zarahemla

FIRST BUILDING SHIPPED THROUGH U.S. MAIL. In 1916, W.H. Coltharp wanted to build a bank in Vernal, Utah, using textured brick. He needed 80,000 bricks. The closest available source was in Salt Lake City, only 150 miles as the crow flies but 427 miles away using the only existing roads in those days. The shipping cost was four times the cost of the bricks! The route was by way of railroad to Mack, Colorado, and then to the narrow-gauge Uintah Railroad and on to Watson, Utah. At Watson, horse-drawn wagons hauled the bricks 65 miles over the Book Cliff Mountains and by way of a cable ferry over the Green River. Brother Coltharp decided that by sending the bricks by U.S. mail, the same routes would be taken but the shipping costs would be cut in half. However, the packages could be no more than 50 pounds each. So, he ordered his 40 tons of brick in 50-pound packages and had them loaded on the train. Normally the Denver and Rio Grande Railroad slowed to throw off mail sacks, but Coltharps' shipment forced a complete stop as tons were unloaded. This threw the entire rail system off schedule. Eventually the bricks arrived, the bank was built, and all was well. Stop by in Vernal and see for yourself—the only building ever shipped through U.S. mail. (William Dempsey, Glendora, CA)

MEDICINE

TOM SMART, *DESERET NEWS*

Michelle Funk was underwater for 66 agonizing minutes.

LONGEST UNDERWATER SUBMERGENCE AND SURVIVAL. During a family picnic in 1986, 2½-year-old Michelle Funk slipped into the frigid river of a nearby stream and remained trapped for a terrifying one hour and six minutes. Clinically she was dead, but the faith of a mother proved otherwise. "The only thing I remember is waking up and my father sticking his tongue out at me," Michelle recalled of the incident. "And it took me a while but I was able to stick my tongue back out at him." Having returned in 2006 from serving in the Franklin, Massachusetts mission, Michelle is doing very well. "I think there is a certain obligation that I hold in my heart, that I know that I shouldn't be here and it's a gift." (KUTV.com, 2/12/06)

LONGEST NONSTOP CPR (1979 WORLD RECORD). In 1979, David Burnham was the assistant director of the JFK Hospital Ambulance/Paramedic Services Department in Palm Beach, California. He was also the volunteer chairman of the Safety Services for the Palm Beach Red Cross Chapter. Brother Burnham decided to unite the two organizations in sponsoring a world record breaking CPR marathon. With dozens of volunteers, Brother Burnham launched the event at the bandstand in nearby Lake Worth Park. Each volunteer performed ten-minute "sprints" of CPR on a mannequin and kept it going uninterrupted for more than 120 hours (5 days), setting a new world record. (Author's interview with David Burnham, 12/5/04)

BEST PLACE TO DIE. In 2004, Utah ranked first in a *Forbes* magazine survey of the best places to die in the United States. The list ranked states according to how they placed on five main criteria: health care quality, legal protection, estate taxes, how many people use hospice, and whether people are likely to die in their homes, at nursing homes, or in a hospital. Utah's first-place ranking was due primarily to strong family ties and the time people take to care for their loved ones. (*Daily Universe*, 9/3/04)

COLLECTIBLES

MOST EXPENSIVE CLOTHING. The most offered for articles of clothing once belonging to early members of the Church was $500,000 for items worn by Hyrum Smith at the time of his martyrdom at Carthage Jail in 1844. The clothing remains in private hands. (Author)

HYMNAL. On December 5, 2006, a rare 1835 hymnal in mint condition sold at an auction for $273,600. It was believed to be the third highest price ever paid for an LDS book. Christie's Auction House did the preliminary research and found that only two other copies of the hymnal on record—both imperfect and one very defective. The buyer and seller were both kept confidential, although the seller said the book was "property of a gentleman." (*Deseret News*, 12/6/06)

ROCKS AND THE EARTH

LONGEST POLISHED SHAFT OF GRANITE (1905 WORLD RECORD). According to the Vermont tourism website, and an interview with the quarry owner from which the shaft was quarried, the largest polished shaft of granite in the world is that sculpted for the Joseph Smith monument in Sharon, Vermont. The single-block of granite obelisk was dedicated on the 100th anniversary of the birth of Joseph Smith, and it stands 38-1/2 feet tall, a foot for each year

CURTIS R. ALLEN

Above: Elaine F. Allen, Lakeview Ward, Bountiful Utah Central Stake, poses to give the Joseph Smith Memorial in Vermont some perspective.

Left: A stonesman works on the base of the obelisk erected in honor of Joseph Smith's 100th birthday. The monument stands at Joseph Smith's birthplace in Sharon, Vermont. The title page of the Book of Mormon was the source for the inscriptions.

FILE PHOTO

of the Prophet's life. It weighs 40 tons and for a shaft that size, only the flawless Vermont granite would do. (Curtis R. Allen, 12/6/04; www.vmga. org/windsor/joesmith.html)

OLDEST ANYTHING ON EARTH. Aside from an ancient meteorite, the oldest anything on earth can be found on the Canadian Shield, a 3-million-square-mile U-shaped region of eastern and central Canada that reaches as far south as the Great Lakes. This was the first part of the North American crustal plate to be raised above sea level about 4.5 billion years ago. The mountains that once stood here have been long gone due to erosion, and the oldest rock from below has now been pushed to the surface. Much of the Shield is covered with a thin layer of soil that supports conifer forests and tundra. Thousands of lakes and outcroppings of bare rock are common. When road crews route a new highway, the backhoes can't break the solid rock just feet beneath the surface and blasting is a necessity. Good friend Steve Harvey of Brockville Branch, Kingston Ontario Canada District, had a chance to visit the oldest place on earth, and sent these samples (see photos). Holding a rock that is

4 billion years old plays strange tricks on your brain. Unless you live near the Canadian Shield, such a rock is older than anything else in life—older than that pizza box under your bed, older than the dirt in the garden, older than any rock you can find, and certainly older than the dinosaurs. While these shield rocks just sat there for billions of years, everything else on earth underwent multiple destructions and formations. And yet we are tempted to set

PAUL B. SKOUSEN

Touching 4 billion years. Annie the Dog (above) gives consideration to these samples of the world's oldest rocks while Brother Paul (right) contemplates the same. Brother Paul speculates that if rocks were nature loving philosophers, they would say, "Thoreau me." But no, the most I got out of them was, "Put me down."

PAUL B. SKOUSEN

aside all of that "as old as the hills" talk to consider and ponder this canine conundrum—is Annie the Dog, pictured here (previous page, left), staring cross-eyed at 4 billion years of rock, or would that be 28 billion in dog years? (Author)

PADDY DOYLE

Don't try this at home! Paddy Doyle of Birmingham, England, strains through to the end of a five-hour endurance event for one-armed pushups. Official rules required that he elect which arm to use, and he could not switch. His new world record for one-armed push-ups in 5 hours is 8,794. Paddy holds 154 national and world fitness records that he has set over the past 20 years. He is the featured athlete in a new section of this book called "Worldwide World Records" that will include people of all faiths or none at all, whose wonderful achievements amaze and inspire us all. Among Paddy's records are the most push-ups in a year (just over 1,500,000) and winning the crown as the World's Fittest Athlete in 2005 when he set the fastest time to complete a 12-mile run, 12-mile walk, 1,250 push-ups, 1,250 star jumps, 3,250 sit-up crunches, 1,250 standing hip flexors, 110 miles cycling, 20 miles rowing, 20 miles cross trainer, upper body weightlifting totaling 300,000 pounds, and a 2-mile swim, all in the amazing time of only 18 hours 56 minutes and 9 seconds! See his complete list of records at the end of the Sports section.

SPORTS

MORMON ACHIEVEMENTS BY THE NUMBERS

1—LDS Women's World Arm Wrestling champion

69—Days to run across the U.S. by an LDS woman

255—Marathons run in a lifetime by a Mormon (and still counting!)

1,500—Meters swam by a 3-year-old

TRACK

MOST WINNING LDS TRACK COACH. When BYU's track and field coach Clarence Robison, Grandview South Utah Stake, passed away in September 2006, he left behind not only a powerhouse track team recognized across the U.S. but also an amazing legacy of achievement that crossed 40 years of excellence: 100 all-Americans, 20 Olympians, one national championship, 9 top-10 finishes in NCAA championships, 19 Western Athletic Conference championships, American and world record holders, and induction into the U.S. Track Coaches Hall of Fame. And in 2004, BYU's new world-class track facility was named after him, the Clarence Robison Stadium. Coach

BYU NEWSNET

Track and field coaches Willard Hirschi, Clarence Robison, and Sherald James in 1974.

Robison was 6–3 in his prime and after serving in World War II, he made the 1948 Olympic team, representing the U.S. in the 5,000-meter run. He lost to the great Emil Zatopek, but the following year, he toured with the U.S. national team in Europe and won 12 of his 16 races. And when the world record for the mile was 4:01, Coach Robison ran it in 4:10. He was a gifted athlete himself and turned BYU from an unknown regional name into a consistent top-20 championship team. (*Deseret News*, 10/2/06)

For a more complete list of athletic achievements, see the master record.

100 METER

100 meter, Men. Leonard Myle-Mills set his personal best at 9.98 seconds.

100 yard, Men over 70. Homer Leman, Phoenix, AZ, 12.5 seconds.

100 yard, Women over 70. Lily McLead Bell, Santiago, Chile, 19 seconds.

400 METER

400 meter, Men. Canagasabi Kunalan, Singapore, 46.9 seconds.

440 yard, Girls 12–13. Lezla Peterson, Saratoga, CA, 57.5 seconds.

800 METER

880 yard, Men. Wade Bell, 1:46.1

800 meter, Men. Ryan Jones, BYU, took first place for the 800 meter-run with a time of 1:53.68. He was competing at the 2007 USA Track and Field High Performance Sprint and Power Meet held at BYU on June 2, 2007.

800 meter, Women. Shawna Halford, Cottonwood High, Utah, 2:09.00 in 1992.

800 meter, Girls (15–18). Heidi Magill, Mountain View High, Utah, 2:06.74 in 2003.

1600 METER/ MILE

Mile, Men. Doug Padilla, 3:54.2 in 1989.

Mile, Men. Jay Woods, 3:54.50 in 1983.

Mile, Women. Susan Nielsen ran the indoor mile in 2004 with a time of 4:43.

1600 meter Relay, Men. Lt. Jack Yerman, Berkeley, CA, 46.14 seconds for the first leg of a 3:02.2 world-record-setting finish.

1000 / 1500 / 3000 METER

1000 meter, Men. Wade Bell, 2:18.7 in 1967.

1500 meter, Men. Paul Cummings, 3:37.6 in 1979.

3000 meter, Men. Doug Padilla, 7:35.84 in 1991.

3000 meter, Women. Nicole Birk, 9:13.2 in 1992.

3000 meter, Boys (11–12). Joshua Rohatinsky, Provo, UT, 9:50:00 in 1994.

3000 meter Steeplechase, Men. BYU steeplechase champion Josh Mc-
Adams won the 2007 U.S. Track and Field Championships in Indianapolis on June 24, 2007, with a time of 8:24.46. The win qualified
him for the world meet in Osaka, Japan, on August 25–September
2, 2007. (BYU NewsNet, 6/26/07)

5000 / 10,000 METER

10,000 meter, Women. Tara Rohatinsky holds the best LDS time with
33:27.

5000 meter, Men. Doug Padilla, 13:29.50 in 1990.

10,000 meter, Men. Ed Eyestone, 27:39.5 in 1986.

10,000 meter, Women. Leanne Whitesides, 34:06.8 in 1992.

LONG DISTANCE AND MARATHONS

CROSS COUNTRY CHAMP. Chelsea (Smith)
McKell, BYU–Hawaii 10th Ward, achieved
something extraordinary by winning the 2004
NCAA Division II cross country championship—she became only the fifth woman to win
two national titles in Division II. Her first win
came in 2003 in North Carolina when she left
the field behind at least 30 seconds. In 2004, at
the championships in Evansville, Indiana, she
fought a sloppy, muddy course to lead for most
of the race and barely squeaked out her win by
just 3 seconds ahead of the second-place winner.
That achievement also won her the selection as
NCAA II National Women's Cross Country
Runner of the Year honors from coaches voting
nationwide. She transferred to BYU in 2005

NEW YORK RUNNERS

Chelsea (Smith) McKell
was the NCAA II women's
runner of the year in 2004.

and led the women's team during her senior year to high national and individual rankings. (*Church News,* 12/4/04; www.byucougars.com)

FIRST WOMAN TO RUN ACROSS THE U.S. They call her the Galloping
Granny or Marathon Mavis, and Sister Mavis Hutchison has earned it. At age
81, and a member of the Vereeniging Ward, Bedfordview South Africa Stake,
Sister Hutchison was still running and winning. In 1978 Mavis earned her
most enduring fame by running across the United States—from Los Angeles

MAVIS HUTCHISON

Mavis Hutchison ran across the U.S. in 69 days.

to New York in 69 days, 2 hours, and 40 minutes, for a total distance of 2,871 miles. "It was my greatest ambition, but I felt so apprehensive," she told *Ensign* magazine. "Would I really be able to do it?" With two vans escorting the 53-year-old, she headed out at 4 AM each day and ran 14 hours a day, stopping only for food. Her journey took her through 13 states and four time zones, and she rotated through 25 pairs of running shoes, which during the trek required 40 repairs. On May 20, 1978, she completed her run at a few minutes before noon. The trip took about 6 million footsteps. The run was a time for her to consider the messages that LDS missionaries had delivered to her earlier. At the end of her run, she knew her answer. Four months later, she was baptized. While training in South Africa to run across the U.S., she set an endurance record that still stands, covering 5,000 kilometers in 69 days, an average of 72 kilometers each day. She also set a record for the farthest distance in a 24-hour period. At age 46, on August 27–28, 1971, Sister Hutchison ran 106 miles 736 yards in 24 hours on a track at Johannesburg. This amazing lifetime of running for Mavis, that remains a part of her eighth decade on earth, has to do with goals. "We have to have goals when you get to my age. You don't grow old; when you stop growing you are old. I don't want to stop growing yet." (*Church News*, 3/18/06; *Ensign*, 1/80; masterstrack.com/blog/000519.html)

MARATHON, FASTEST—MEN. In the Chicago Marathon, Ed Eyestone ran a personal best at 2:10:59.

MARATHON, FASTEST—WOMEN. In 2004, Maggie Chan-Roper ran a personal best at the Salt Lake Marathon in 2:35.

MOST ACCOMPLISHED MARATHON RUNNER. John Bozung, Orem, Utah, is to date the most accomplished marathon and distance runner on record, as demonstrated with the records that follow.

• **Most Consecutive Marathons, Weekly.** John Bozung set a great goal for his 52nd birthday year: 52 marathons in 52 weeks. This amazing string of endurance and stamina comes on the heels of having already run the 26.2 mile run more than 200 times in all 50 states and on all seven continents. In fact, he is only the second person to run marathons on all seven conti-

JOHN BOZUNG

nents. He has run in some amazing places, including among flocks of amazed penguins in Antarctica and a run that finished inside the original Olympic Stadium in Athens, Greece. His only win so far came in the Himalayas at an altitude of 21,000 feet—a feat he achieved in 4 hours 25 minutes. For most marathons he averages around 3 hours 2 minutes. (Author's interview, 2/20/06; *Deseret News*, 8/17/05)

• **Most Consecutive Marathons, Monthly.** John Bozung is setting an unofficial world record for the most consecutive months of running at least one marathon a month. He's been at it for about 14 years and as of September 2007, he's at 168. There is nothing stopping him, so for the record's sake, just add one more for each month since September 2007. (Author's interview, 9/21/07)

JOHN BOZUNG

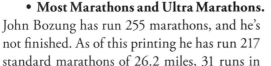

John Bozung on the trail outside of Dallas in 2004.

• **Most Marathons and Ultra Marathons.** John Bozung has run 255 marathons, and he's not finished. As of this printing he has run 217 standard marathons of 26.2 miles, 31 runs in 50 kilometer races, one run that was 35 miles, nine 50-mile runs, two 62-mile runs (100K), and one 100-mile run. (Author's interview, 9/21/07)

JOHN BOZUNG

John Bozung stops at Checkpoint Charlie in Germany

• **First LDS to Run a Marathon on all 7 Continents.** John Bozung became the second person in human history in 1997 to run a marathon on all seven continents in one year, and he would have been first had a competitor not heard of his goal and rushed to beat him. Among the seven run that year are included the highest overall marathon at the Mt. Everest Challenge in the Himalayas on the Nepal-India border, averaging 12,000 feet in elevation. He also ran the world's lowest marathon in the Death Valley Marathon. The most northern is on the north shore of Baffin Island, about 400 miles south of the Arctic Circle at the Nanisvik Marathon that ran through Arctic Bay. The most southern marathon in the world is on King George Island in Antarctica.

- Antarctica Marathon on King George Island, Antarctica, on February 18, 1997 (time: 3:04:22)
- Mount Kilimanjaro Marathon in Moshi, Tanzania, Africa, on June 29, 1997 (time: 3:47:15)
- Nanisivik Midnight Sun Marathon in Nanisivik, Baffin Island, Northwest Territories, Canada, North America, on July 6, 1997 (time: 4:14:26)
- Liberator Marathon, Caracas, Venezuela, South America, on July 20, 1997 (time 3:33:30)
- Noosa Marathon, Noosa, Queensland, Australia, on September 31, 1997 (time: 3:27:47)
- Athens Marathon Athens, Greece, Europe, on October 26, 1997 (time: 3:19:59) and his on way to Asia stopped for the Delta Lloyd Marathon in Amsterdam on November 2, 1997 (time: 3:17:08)
- Mt. Everest Challenge Marathon, Darjeeling, India, Asia, on November 8, 1997 (time: 4:43:40, 1st place)

(Author's interview, 9/21/07)

MOST BOSTON MARATHONS. It's an amazing streak by anybody's standard. Beginning in April 1979, Richard J. Carling, Monument Park

RICHARD CARLING

Boston Baked Being? 29 going on 30 Boston Marathons in a row by Richard Carling.

17th Ward, Monument Park North Stake, started a string of consecutive years running the Boston Marathon that stands as of this writing at 29, the last being April 16, 2007, and qualified to run his 30th in April 2008. He has run in more than 120 marathons over his lifetime, running his best in 1982 with a time of 2:33:21, performed at age 44. His best Boston Marathon time is 2:41:37, run in 1981. Brother Carling's running has taken him all over America (literally!)—from Boston to Honolulu and from the Fiesta Bowl to San Francisco, with stops in between. (Author's interview, 6/25/07)

BEST CONSECUTIVE MARATHON TIME. Who can claim the best consecutive sub-2:30 marathon times within two weeks? In 2003, Alexander Pachev, Slate Canyon 3rd Ward, Provo Utah Stake, ran a marathon on September 30, 2003, with a time of 2:27:46. Two weeks later, he ran even better at 2:24:47. (Alexander Pachev, 3/28/06)

MARATHON BOYS. Some fantastically talented young marathon runners are growing up in the Church. These records date back a few years but reflect some amazing achievements at early ages.

- **5 years old**—Kevin Strain, Grants Pass, Oregon, 6:56:39 (1972)
- **6 years old**—Kevin Strain, Grants Pass, Oregon, 4:15:02 (1973)
- **7 years old**—Kevin Strain, Grants Pass, Oregon, 3:34:30 (1974)
- **8 years old**—Kevin Strain, Grants Pass, Oregon, 3:15:42 (1975)
- **10 years old**—Cameron Linford, Midway 4th Ward, Midway Utah Stake, 3:18:33 (1988)

FLOYD STRAIN

Young marathon champ Kevin Strain leads his younger siblings in a race to the finish.

(Sources: Floyd Strain, Grants Pass, Oregon, 1/3/05; Cameron Linford, 12/1/04)

LONGEST WALKER/RUNNER, MEN. Brian Stubbs, a high priest in the Blanding 4th Ward, Blanding Utah West Stake, estimates he has more than 62,000 documented miles under his belt, er, his feet from a lifetime of running and walking that began at age 13. As a young teen, he began running every day and worked himself up to four miles a day, usually six days a week. In high school, he upped his run to 8–12 miles a day. His mission to the Navajo reservation included a truck, but for six of those months he had to walk, adding another 10–20 miles a day. After his return home, he began his running routine again and averaged 6–8 miles a day, five days a week, up into his 40s. He scaled back to run just

BRIAN STUBBS

Brian Stubbs walks and reads.

for health's sake and as of this writing, at age 58, he still puts on about 1,000 miles of running a year. As a teacher, he enjoys long 15-mile walks up into the local canyons, where he reads and corrects papers and enjoys the scenery—even in winter! At his current pace, he expects to cross the 100,000 mile mark by age 70, and then it's time to rotate the tires, good brother! (Author interview, 10/4/06)

HIGH JUMP / LONG JUMP

HIGH JUMP, MEN (1943 WORLD RECORD). Fred Sheffield, the captain of the 1944 University of Utah basketball team that won the NCAA championship, was also a great high jumper. In 1943 he was the NCAA track and field champ with a jump of 6 feet eight inches. In those days they jumped feet first. He was also the first athlete to place four consecutive years in the NCAA high jump championships. (sportsline.com/collegebasketball)

- **High Jump, Men (2001 Mormon World Record).** Charlie Clinger, Ogden, Utah, 7 feet 8-1/2 inches, in 2001.
- **High Jump, Boys (Age 18).** Tory Bailey, Rupert, ID, 7 feet 1 inches, 1993.
- **High Jump, Girls (Age 15).** Kristin McQuade, Casper, WY, 5 feet 11-1/2 inches.
- **High Jump, Girls (Age 13).** Lori Mertes, Chatworth, CA, 5 feet 6 inches, 1986.

LONGEST STANDING BROAD JUMP. Back in 1972, when mighty leaps from a standstill counted for something, Paul Barnes set a school best, if not a Mormon World Record when he leapt 12 feet 1 inch as a senior on his track team at Highland High School in Salt Lake City, Utah. Brother Barnes is today a member of the Spring City 1st Ward, Mount Pleasant Utah Stake. (Author's interview, 7/19/07)

- **Long Jump, Boys (15–18).** Jared Hansen, Colorado Springs, CO, 25 feet 2 inches.
- **Long Jump, Boys (9).** Jared Passmore, Pleasant Grove, UT, 7 feet 9-3/4 inches.
- **Long Jump, Girls (15).** Melanie Bemis, Canby, OR, 17 feet 2-3/4 inches, 1993.
- **Triple Jump, Girls (15).** Meagan Gable, Buckeye, AZ, 34 feet 8-1/2 inches, 1993

OTHER FIELD EVENTS

HIGHEST POLE VAULT.

• Robison Pratt, BYU, set a new personal best when he cleared the bar at 18 feet 4-3/4 inches in 2006. (gomatadors.onlinesports.com)

• Robert Low, BYU, took first place for the pole vault with a height of 17 feet 2-3/4 inches. He was competing at the 2007 USA Track and Field High Performance Sprint and Power Meet held at BYU on June 2, 2007. (BYU NewsNet, 6/4/07)

LONGEST DISCUS THROW. Niklas Arrhenius, BYU, took first place for the discus throw with a distance of 206-11 feet. He was competing at the 2007 USA Track and Field High Performance Sprint and Power Meet held at BYU on June 2, 2007. (BYU NewsNet, 6/4/07)

WEIGHT THROW (NATIONAL HIGH SCHOOL RECORD, 2004). Leif Arrhenius set an American high school record for the farthest weight throw at 82 feet 10 inches with a 25-pound weight. The object used for a weight throw is a 25-pound plastic ball filled with lead pellets. A metal handle allows the athlete to hold the weight by the handle, spin 2–4 times in a ring and let it fly. The high school shot put is a solid 12-pound ball of iron. (Anders Arrhenius, 2/3/05)

ARRHENIUS FAMILY

JAVELIN, BOYS (12). On July 21, 2006, Aaron Potter, Albany Oregon 3rd Ward, set a U.S. national age-group record with a throw of 178-11, beating the old record by 13 feet. (*Church News*, 8/26/06)

Niklas Arrhenius, a champion discus thrower, is one of several in a talented athletic family who frequently break records in their chosen events.

MULTI-EVENT AND IRONMAN

TRIATHLON CHAMPION, SENIOR MEN. In New Zealand, in 1985, Max Burdick, 62, took first place for men over 60 in New Zealand's Ironman Triathlon. Brother Burdick swam two miles, biked for more than eight hours, and ran for 20 miles to complete the competition in 14 hours 43 minutes. He was a member of the Cottonwood 14th Ward, Salt Lake Big Cottonwood Stake. (*Church News*, 4/28/85)

TRIATHLON CHAMPION, BANTAM GIRLS (9-10). In 1995, Amy Menlove, 10, won the USA Track and Field Association Junior Olympics Region 10 triathlon championship. Her total of 1,030 points tied the region record and broke the Utah state record. Triathlon events include the 200-meter dash, high jump, and shot put. She was a member of the Eastridge 4th Ward, Draper, Utah, Eastridge Stake. (*Church News*, 8/12/95)

JERRY NOBLE

Jerry Noble, national champ in the decathlon.

BEST DECATHLON MARKS, DIVISION II COLLEGE. In May 2001, Jerry R. Noble Jr., Camarillo 1st Ward, Camarillo California Stake, braved wind, rain, and lightning to become the national champion in the decathlon for Division II colleges. He fared well during the events, but when it was time to throw the discuss, a thunderstorm clapped overhead and began pouring rain. All the other athletes headed for cover, leaving Brother Nobel alone on the track. It turns out it was his best discus throw ever! (Jerry R. Noble, 10/19/05)

100 Meters: 10.90
Long Jump: 6.44 meters
16-pound Shot Put: 34'10.50
High Jump: 6'03.25
400 meter: 48.02
110 meter high hurdles: 16.02
Discuss Throw: 118'7.00
Pole Vault: 15'01.00
Javelin Throw: 143'11.00
1500 meter: 4:42.23

JERRY NOBLE

BEST DECATHLON MARKS, MASTERS DIVISION (60–64). The Decathlon is held in various venues around the world. Here are the known LDS Master's Division men's records to date:

100 Meters: 11.1—Robert Gent, Beaver, Utah
Long Jump: 21'6"—Robert Gent, Beaver, Utah
16-pound Shot Put: 38'—Robert Gent, Beaver, Utah
High Jump: 6'—Robert Gent, Beaver, Utah
400 Meters: 51.9—Robert Gent, Beaver, Utah

110 Meter high hurdles: 16.5—Robert Gent, Beaver, Utah
Discus: 125′—Robert Gent, Beaver, Utah
Pole Vault: 11′—Robert Gent, Beaver, Utah
Javelin: 165′—Robert Gent, Beaver, Utah
1500 Meters: 5.01—Robert Gent, Beaver, Utah

IRONMAN COMPETITION. At the Hawaii Ironman World Triathlon competition in 2001, Mark Baker, president of the Muncie Indiana Stake, endured the marathon swim, bike ride, and run to finish with a time of 14:41:41:00. The official Ironman competition involves a 2.4-mile swim that transitions to a 112-mile bike ride, and finishes with a 26.2-mile marathon run. The Ironman Triathlon began in Hawaii as a specific race event and has evolved into a race series, with various qualifying events around the world, culminating in the Hawaii Ironman World Triathlon. To finish the race, a participant must complete the swim and bike ride within the first 10 hours, and cross the finish line for the marathon by the 17-hour mark to be considered an Ironman. Brother Baker embarked on his Ironman goal after reading about the pioneers and wondering if he could do such a thing if he were called upon. He saw the Hawaii Ironman as a way to test himself, not as a replication of the pioneers' trials, but as an extreme test of physical endurance. During the race, he had a unique source of inspiration. "You can actually see the Kona Hawaii Temple many times while you are racing, and seeing Moroni helped me be strong!" Afterward, the experience gave him many opportunities to speak to the youth about "the need for us all to test the limits in life" to improve ourselves, he said. And what do the youth call him? Ironman stake president! (Author's interview, 4/16/06)

MARK BAKER

Mark Baker has the best LDS time for the Hawaii Ironman Triathlon at 14:41:41:00.

FOOTBALL

FIRST LDS NFL HEAD COACH. Andy Reid, Villanova, Pennsylvania, was the first LDS head coach in the NFL when he took over the top job at the Philadelphia Eagles in 1999. He as born in Los Angeles and played

FILE PHOTO

Andy Reid

offensive guard and tackle for BYU until graduation in 1981. For 17 years he moved around to several universities, and in 1992 he took over the offensive assistant slot for the Green Bay Packers. An opening at the Eagles came in 1997 where he was quarterbacks coach and assistant head coach. As head coach for the Eagles, he led his team to four NFC Championships from 2001 to 2004, winning the NFC Championship in 2004. He's been honored as the Coach of the Year twice and holds the most successful win record in team history. To his credit, he's won five division titles and four trips to the NFC championships. The unheralded genius behind the team's success was Brother Reid's team-building and character-building expertise. Said player Hiro Tanaka, "He took a bunch of kids of different races and combined them into making a team. We never had a problem." Another player, Jim Sartoris, saw the great transition. "I was in that first group, and he came in, took a terrible program and built it back up into a championship team. I was right there for that." And Reid's great college mentor, LaVell Edwards of BYU said, "I saw a man who knew how to treat people. He didn't care who you were, what you were about. At the same time, now, he could crack the whip. He never turned away an autograph seeker. And he didn't lose his cool during tough times." Brother Reid and his wife, Tammy, have five children. (www.philadelphiaeagles.com; various Internet sources)

FIRST LDS NFL QUARTERBACK. Virgil Carter set a high standard for quarterbacks at BYU when he graduated in 1967. During his college playing career, he set 6 NCAA records, 19 Western Athletic Conference (WAC) records, and 24 BYU records. In his junior and senior years he was named All-Conference and WAC Player of the Year for both years. He was an All-American honorable mention, received the Dale Rex Memorial Award in 1967, and was honored for his scholarship as well. He graduated in statistics from the College of Physical and Engineering Sciences with the honor of BYU Outstanding Senior, and for those final two years he was named Scholastic All-American. He went on to earn his MBA. Brother Carter's professional football career ran from 1967 to '76, and he began with the Chicago Bears in 1967. He moved on to the Cincinnati Bengals and then Chicago Fire. He was named captain of the Bengals. Professional honors included leading the NFL in pass completion percentage in 1971 and being named the

BYU SPORTS HALL OF FAME

Virgil Carter, first LDS NFL quarterback.

Most Valuable Player in 1968, 1971, and 1974. Brother Carter married Judy Green in 1967. He retired from professional football in 1976 and has since enjoyed sports broadcasting and making various appearances on radio and television. (www.cougarclub.com; www.pro-football-reference.com)

BASEBALL

FILE PHOTO

Ken Hubbs, first rookie to win a Gold Glove Award.

TOP ROOKIE IN THE MAJOR LEAGUE. Ken Hubbs of Colton, California, became the first LDS Rookie of the Year in 1962 while playing for the Chicago Cubs. He was honored for some amazing ball playing, including setting two major league fielding records at second base (it was the first year he had even played that position), most consecutive games without an error (78), and most chances without an error (418). He was the first rookie ever to win a Gold Glove Award, also in 1962. He was an outstanding athlete and was the first high school athlete to be named All-American in three sports—football, basketball, and baseball. Ken was genuinely modest and humble and was the type of person who challenged himself in all things. He fought his fear of flying by earning his pilot's license in 1964. Flying with friend Dennis Dayle near Provo, Utah, on a stormy February day, he had just taken off for his trip home to Colton, California, when his plane crashed on the frozen Utah Lake. Both were killed, but his sterling life has been a source of inspiration for sports writers and historians ever since. (John Buckles interview; NYT, 2/16/64; www.baseball-reference.com)

SWIMMING/DIVING

LONGEST NONSTOP SWIMMING RELAY. Six swimmers took the "Open 24 Hours" sign pretty literally at the Newark YMCA where they set a world record for swimming 10 days straight in a nonstop relay. It all began August 14, 1979, when Matt Howard, a member of the Rose Valley Ward, Peoria, Arizona Stake, and five other competitive swimmers began taking 60-minute turns to swim a minimum of 100 laps per turn. On August 24, 1919, the exhausted swimmers stood, or bobbed, at the finish line of a 469.57-mile-in-240-hours accomplishment. The feat wasn't recognized by Guinness until 2003 when persistent efforts to claim their title came to fruition as Guinness World Records made the record official. (Matt Howard, 11/22/04)

BARNES FAMILY

In 2005, Richard Barnes became the first Mormon man to swim the English Channel. The frigid challenge took him almost 17 hours.

FIRST TO SWIM ENGLISH CHANNEL, MEN. On the official list of "successful swims" across the English Channel, number 719 just happens to be Latter-day Saint Richard Barnes, 33, of the 16th Ward, Sandy Utah Granite South Stake. To put Brother Barnes's achievement in perspective, more than 1,500 people have climbed Mount Everest! Richard completed his channel swim on August 6, 2005, in 16 hours and 43 minutes. However, because of contrary currents, he actually swam 36 miles, an astonishing accomplishment that won him the Greatest Feat of Endurance trophy for the year 2005 by the Channel Swimming Association. Channel swimming is guided by very strict rules. Richard could wear one swim cap, a pair of goggles, and a Speedo-type racing suit. He was allowed to "grease up" with Channel Grease, a mixture of Vaseline and lanolin that helps slightly with the cold water, but helps more with the chafing around the neck and armpits.

Richard trained an entire year for the event and gained 15 pounds for extra body insulation. The water there is cold, and in the summer months it averages 60 degrees. On the day of Richard's swim, it was a dark midnight when he jumped into the 56-degree water with 4-foot waves. While tides, currents, 600 daily trips by huge tankers, 200 daily trips by ferries, ships, fog, choppy seas, wind, and jellyfish stings have ended many a swimmer's best laid plans, the most dangerous threat is hypothermia. Training in cold water is how to combat that, Richard said.

As the swim commenced, Richard was allowed to stop for nourishment and liquids from his support boat, but he couldn't touch it or he would be disqualified. By the fourth hour, he was stopping every 30 minutes or so to drink hot chocolate or Gatorade, and eat canned peaches or pears. He kept his feeding times down to a minute as the tide was constantly pushing him toward the North

BARNES FAMILY

Every Channel swimmer must be careful to avoid jellyfish, whose stings can quickly end a good swim.

BARNES FAMILY

Swimming the English Channel has been accomplished less than 800 times, while climbing Mount Everest has been done more than 1,500 times.

Sea or the Atlantic. Richard was with his brother Dave when they started out, but six hours into the swim, Dave had to drop out. The pair had launched from Shakespeare Beach between Dover and Folkestone, England, and their intent was to land at the closest point in France called Cap Gris Nez. But those currents pushed Richard to a beach near Wissant, France. And so, did he have to worry about sharks? "No, the water is too cold for sharks," Richard said, "which may say something about whether people should even be swimming there in the first place!" (Author's interview, 4/12/06)

FASTEST SWIM ACROSS THE ENGLISH CHANNEL, MEN. On August 26, 2006, David Barnes, 37, became the fastest Latter-day Saint man to swim the 21-mile English Channel, setting a time of 14 hours 1 minute. As noted in the previous record, David made his first try with his brother Richard in 2005 but had to stop six hours into the

event. But this time, he swam it alone and was encouraged by Richard, who joined him in the water at miles 9 and 11, for an hour each time. Aside from being smacked in the face by a jellyfish, David made the trip in record time. Said their father, David Barnes Sr., as David trudged onto the sands of France, "It was a huge moment! I tell them Richard was the first Utahn and the youngest, and David was the oldest and the fastest . . . they both set records." (Author's interview; *Deseret News*, 9/10/06)

Above: Official rules deny swimmers anything more than goggles, skull cap, racing suit, and Channel Grease to battle the cold. Any extra insulation for warmth must be grown or gained!
Right: David nears the end of his swim with the French coast happily in view!

BARNES FAMILY

FIRST BROTHERS TO SWIM THE ENGLISH CHANNEL. On August 6, 2005, Richard Barnes (left), 33, 16th Ward, Sandy Utah Granite South Stake, swam the English Channel in 16 hours and 43 minutes. On August 26, 2006, his brother David Barnes (right), 37, achieved the same feat in 14 hours one minute. (Author's interview; *Deseret News*, 9/10/06)

BARNES FAMILY

HOROMONA FAMILY

Korbyn Horomona, champion swimmer at age 3.

LONGEST SWIM, 3-YEAR-OLD (2007 WORLD RECORD). It was a breathtaking achievement, literally, by any standard as 3-year-old Korbyn Horomona, Helensvale Ward, Gold Coast Australia Stake, set a new world record for distance swimming for her age group. Her parents started her swimming at age 2 for safety reasons, and within a year, her swimming coach believed the young protégé could break 1,000 meters if she worked at it. After training toward that goal, she was cheered on by family and admiring supporters as she completed the last lap for the 1,000-meter mark. And then instead of stopping, she just kept going, to everyone's astonishment. For an unstopping 90 minutes, she kept up her freestyle and backstroke until finishing 1.5 kilometers. (*Church News,* 4/21/07)

LONGEST NONSTOP WATER TREAD. In 1973 Charlie Roberts was a skinny 135-pounder who thought he'd take BYU's challenge to see who could stay in the water the longest. A group of about 40 signed up. Brother Roberts recalls hearing the record was held by a British woman at 24 hours, so his goal was to at least match that. After treading water for 24 hours and 48 minutes, all but one of the other 40 competitors had given up. He said, "I could see there was one competitor in the 250-pound range that was going to outlast me, so I called it a night." Brother Roberts and his family live in Tooele, Utah, where he recently served as mayor. (Author's interview, 12/07/04)

SCHOOL SPIRIT

BEST DRILL TEAM IN THE U.S. The Skyline High School (Salt Lake City) drill team of 20 girls, 18 of whom were LDS, won the national championship at the 1981 Miss Drill Team competition in Los Angeles. The team captured the best "prop precision" title, plus dance, military, and novelty precision championship awards and the prestigious Producers Award. Their coach, Pam Jensen, worked miracles, according to Gloria Wright, mother of the twin Wright girls. "She was a real martinet, and taught those girls everything there is to know about commitment." (Author's interview, 3/12/05)

DESERET NEWS

Best Drill Team in America included 18 LDS, four of whom are (l-r) (married names) Shannon Brimhall Reynolds, Cynthia Nelson Knight, and twins Martha Wright McKay and Rebecca Wright Phillips.

CHEER AND DANCE CHAMPS. In April 2007, BYU's Cougarettes won their

BYUCOUGARETTES.COM

BYU Cougarettes won seven national championships in 10 years.

seventh national title and their second 3-peat in ten years. The largest Division 1A college cheer and dance competition pitted squads from all across the nation. The Cougarettes won the National Collegiate College Dance Team National Championship in 1997, 1998, 1999, 2001, 2005, 2006, and 2007. (www.byucougarettes.com)

WRESTLING

WRESTLING—UNDEFEATED COLLEGE CHAMPION.
Cael Sanderson, originally of Heber, Utah, achieved the remarkable record of going undefeated during his career at Iowa State University. He stepped onto the mat 159 times, and stepped off a winner every time, including four national championship matches. He was the first college wrestler ever to win four NCAA titles with an undefeated record. Nicknamed "The Heber Creamer," he was featured in *Sports Illustrated* and on ESPN. He was honored with an ESPY, and was named NCAA Most Outstanding Wrestler four times. He even had a Congressional resolution written in his honor, and later received a congratulatory handshake from the president of the United States. (*Church News,* 3/30/02)

IOWA STATE UNIVERSITY

Cael Sanderson's college wrestling record is 159–0. He is now head wrestling coach at Iowa State.

SUMO WRESTLING. The most successful LDS sumo wrestler is Kelly Gneiting of the Window Rock Ward, Chinle Arizona Stake, who is the two-time U.S. National Heavyweight Champion. In 2006, he represented the U.S. at the World Sumo Championships and came in third. At 6 feet even, and a weight that varies from a healthy 405–420 pounds, Brother Gneiting packs a real wallop when it comes to the most ancient of all competitive sports. "Sumo came before karate, judo, and jujitsu," he told reporters, and explained that the goal isn't to simply bounce off your opponent. There are more than 60 winning techniques called "kimarite" that help an athlete conquer an opponent who might weigh more than himself. Gneiting is married with four children, and in September 2006, he was invited to film a scene for *Ocean's Thirteen* starring Al Pacino, George Clooney, Brad Pitt, and the gang. Pacino's character hosts a sumo wrestling match in his casino, and during filming, both Pacino and Clooney were

PEOPLE'S DAILY ONLINE

Kelly Gneiting (left) is a two-time US national Heavyweight Champion.

watching. "It wasn't acting," Gneiting told the *Deseret News*, but "it was fun. . . . These movie stars were watching me sumo wrestle; that was a crazy experience." (*Church News*, 7/22/06; *Deseret News*, 1/11/07; www. planetjh.com)

MARTIAL ARTS

MOST ICE CRACKED WITH HAND OR HEAD (1997 WORLD RECORD). Sam Alma Kuoha, Granite Hills Ward, El Cajon California Stake, was already the youngest karate grandmaster in the world by 1988. He held a 10th-degree black belt in Chinese Kempo-style karate. He is perhaps the most publicized martial artist alive with more than 35 magazine covers, 150 featured articles, and induction into various martial arts halls of fame 11 times. His amazing power and skill led him to new world records in breaking ice.

JAY LENO, NBC, AND SAM KUOHA

- **1978 World Record.** In April 1978, he broke 4,200 pounds of ice with one hand, setting a new world record.
- **1979 World Record.** In May 1979, he set an endurance record by breaking 4,950 pounds of ice stacked in blocks of 600 to 1,500 pounds, in 3 minutes 17 seconds, setting a new world record.
- **1979 World Record.** He broke 1,500 pounds with his forehead, setting another new world record.

(LDS, 7/30/88; John DeWitt, 4/23/07)

JAY LENO, NBC, AND SAM KUOHA

Top: Sam Alma Kuoha holds several world records for ice breaking, and broke 2,150 pounds on Jay Leno's *Tonight Show.* Below: Brother Kuoha visits with Leno and guests.

JAY LENO, NBC, AND SAM KUOHA

Sam Alma Kuoha's students and associates who joined him to visit Jay Leno. From l-r bottom: Sensei John DeWitt, Sempai Alfred Parker, Sensei Tim Spendley and Sensei Cosmo Chiles (co-designer). Top from l-r, Robbie Gibson (co-designer), Sensei Jeff Hayes, Jay Leno, Grandmaster Sam Kuoha, Rick Chiles, Shihan Ben Kahananui, Sensei Jamey Gibson and Sensei Al Parker, Security.

JAY LENO, NBC, AND SAM KUOHA

Live on the *Tonight Show*: Brother Kuoha smashes the old world record by cracking 16 feet of ice with a single blow with his forehead.

KARATE BLACK BELT, YOUNGEST, BOYS. It's a race! Quite a number of young Latter-day Saints have earned their black belts. Here are the youngest stalwarts so far:

- **Age 9 years 1 month**—Josh DeLoach, Delta 5th Ward, Delta Utah Stake (earned October 1992)
- **Age 9 years 9 months**—Steven Waldron, Silverbell Ward, Tucson Arizona West Stake (earned December 1, 2001)

KARATE, WORLD CHAMPION—YOUNGEST. In November 1994, Josh DeLoach, Delta 5th Ward, Delta Utah Stake, won the world title in New Jersey at age 10. Josh's specialty was choreographed fighting. To win he had to compete against world class competitors, defeating both juniors and adults. In fact, he was the youngest competitor in his division of 17 and under. When his name was announced, the whole audience cheered; they were pulling for this amazing youngster who held up so well against other boys several years older than he. He went on to earn 10 Utah state titles in karate and two Ed Parker international titles, and he served a full-time mission in Puebla, Mexico. (Author's interview, 10/1/07)

JOSH DELOACH
DELOACH FAMILY

Josh DeLoach, world champion 1994.

YOUNGEST KARATE BLACK BELT—GIRLS (1999 WORLD RECORD). On February 16, 1999, Jessi Rivera of the Haywards Heath Ward, Crawley England Stake, became the youngest girl in the world to earn her black belt in karate at age 7. She was featured on CNN with some of her karate classmates, and her achievement was broadcast around the world. She began

RIVERA FAMILY

training at age 3, having been inspired by her mom, dad, and brother Colin who also took up the sport. It turns out she was a natural even at that tender young age. When she graduated from white belt to red belt, she was so little and shy that her Sensei (instructor) had to grade her while standing behind a stack of chairs where he watched through cracks so as not to make her too nervous! Sister Fiona Rivera, also a black belt, asked Jessi on the morning of her black belt grading if she was worried about anything. "Yes," Jessi quietly confessed, "I am worried that I won't be able to memorize all the articles of faith by my baptism." (Author's interview, 1/10/08)

CYCLING

BEST BMX CYCLIST—MEN. In the BMX world, Mike Aitken is one of the most familiar faces and stylists in the sport. He has appeared on countless magazine covers and in documentaries, advertising videos, and stills, and his amazing air-grabbing hang time is all over YouTube. Brother Aitken is always on the move but calls Utah his home. He began racing at age 11, and in 1995 he was ranked number one in Utah. He moved into stunts, and with just his own legs for pedal power, he could make 5–6 major jumps on an obstacle course with 25–30-foot gaps between jump. He can do 360- and 720-degree spins, back flips, tailwhips, and a lot more

MIKE AITKEN

while up in the air. Mike is a favorite at the X Games and Gravity Games. He took first in the world in 2004 and routinely ranks among the top 4. He has his own signature bike parts, and various sponsors are always looking for his endorsement. And he loves it. "Keep it simple and have fun," he said. "Don't get too stressed about sponsors. Live life and ride your bike." Married in 2005, he and his wife reside a few miles outside of Salt Lake City. (Ann Aitken [Mike's amazed and admiring mom!], 1/3/05)

LORI MARTIN

Arielle Martin in action!

BEST BMX CYCLIST—WOMEN. Arielle Martin grew up on bicycles, taking her first solo ride without training wheels at age 2-1/2. By age 5 she entered her first BMX race, and by age 10 she was nationally ranked. At age 15, with four Number One national titles behind her, she became the youngest girl pro on the 2000 ABA BMX circuit. When she was 16, a severe accident fractured her back, and doctors said she was done with athletics. After a blessing, she began improving and defied the doctors and regained her strength and agility. She's still ranked high among women BMX cyclists and is the second woman in the world to land a back flip successfully on her bike. She and her husband live in Clarksville, Tennessee. (Lori Martin, 12/21/04; www.go211.com/u/bmxdiva)

FASTEST CROSS-COUNTRY BICYCLING TRIP—13-YEAR-OLD. In June 1962, Dean Millman of Sunset, Utah, embarked on a cross country trip to New York at age 13. Riding a new Huffy 10-speed that was too tall for him, even with the seat lowered all the way, Dean launched his adventure with vigor. For the first few days, he managed 150 miles a day but partway across Wyoming, a police officer spotted him and invited him to stay the night in the local firehouse. Dean proved a hit with the firemen, who then called ahead to the next town on Dean's itinerary and arranged for him to spend the night in the firehouse there. Suddenly, towns all across the nation were vying for him to spend the night in their firehouse. At each stop he was awarded honorary fire and police deputy badges. The press loved the story and followed him all the way. At the end of his 2,500-mile ride to see a friend in New York, the popular game show *To Tell the Truth* had him make an appearance, one of the youngest ever to do so. The network paid for Dean's flight home to

DEAN MILLMAN

Dean Millman begins his cross-country trip.

Utah. Dean later traded his bicycling adventures for paintbrush and canvas and developed a brilliant painting career. This was cut short when he succumbed to leukemia in 1977, but to this day those who knew Dean and his painting skills still remember the young man who at age 13 took on a nation single-handedly. (Author's interview, Neil Millman, September 2007)

FASTEST CROSS-COUNTRY BICYCLING TRIP— 17-YEAR-OLD. In the summer of 1967, Pat Casaday, now of the Crescent Ridge 6th Ward, Sandy Utah Crescent Ridge Stake, embarked on a 2,600-mile adventure that took him from Utah through 32 states in 53 days, visiting the southwestern, southern, and northern states. Averaging 120–130 miles a day except Sundays, Pat and his riding buddy, Craig Nelson, also of Salt Lake City, wore out three pairs of tires and had to be innovative when it came to sleeping at night. With only $100 to spend on food, lodging, and emergencies, they depended on the good-heartedness of people along the way. On several occasions, a kind LDS bishop let them sleep on the living room floor. And when things were desperate, a local sheriff usually let them spend the night in the town jail. Other good Samaritans helped them with food, a little spending money, sometimes a good steak dinner "on the house." They were arrested in Texas as suspected runaways.

PAT CASSIDY

Pat Casady begins his 2,600-mile journey.

"We usually bought one meal a day and had two given to us," Pat told the press. "It was a humbling experience . . . hoping we would meet someone who would come help us." And that help was always forthcoming. (Author's interview, 12/24/04)

LARGEST MASS CYCLING RIDE THROUGH TAIWAN. In July and August of 2006, at least 2,500 Latter-day Saints with friends and local missionaries helped celebrate the 50th anniversary of missionary work in that country by riding 250 miles up both coasts. Teams of cyclists began at the southern tip and split into groups that rode various segments up the east and west coasts. The riders made it a goodwill trip, passing out literature and flags, shaking hands, and spreading goodwill. (*Church News*, 8/12/06)

GUY HANSEN

Guy Hansen on what could be the world's smallest unicycle, his 2-1/2-inch "Giraffe."

GUY HANSEN

Family of unicyclists in 1993 (l-r): Guy, Brian, Willy, Melissa, Morgan, Karen, and Alex. The family regularly participates in parades, timed-speed events, endurance events, and much more.

GUY HANSEN

Karen and Guy Hansen

UNICYCLE, HAND PEDALING DISTANCE (WORLD RECORD 2004). On April 17, 1999, Guy Hansen, Lindon 1st Ward, Lindon Utah Central Stake, set a distance record for farthest nonstop unicycle pedaled by hand (not feet!) at 1,572 feet. (Guy Hansen, 2/15/06)

UNICYCLE, HAND PEDALING SPEED (WORLD RECORD 2004). On April 17, 1999, Guy Hansen, Lindon 1st Ward, Lindon Utah Central Stake, set a speed record for hand pedaling a unicycle at 8.5 miles per hour. (Guy Hansen, 2/15/06)

GOLF

LONGEST TIME PLAYING MINIATURE GOLF. Brigham Young University's Professional Miniature Golf Association had two goals in mind on February 18, 2005: to raise money for the Kids Cause Foundation and to set a world record for playing miniature golf 24 hours straight. One Utah business agreed to pay $1 for every hole played. By the beginning of the final round, 504 holes had been played. Tired and delirious, Todd Jacobs, a member of the team, said, "If someone beats our record, we'll be right back out there." Oh, and one more thing . . . Guinness has a new record that didn't exist before. (Deseretnews.com, 02/21/05)

MOST PUBLIC GOLF COURSES PLAYED IN A STATE. At age 18, Rod Peterson, Jordan River 3rd Ward, Jordan River Ridge Utah Stake, golfed all 83 public golf courses in the state of Utah. From Smithfield to Kanab, and from Wendover to Vernal, he's played them all—literally. He told the *Salt Lake Tribune* that his best course was clearly St. George's Sunbrook. The worst was Belmont Springs in northern Utah's Plymouth. "Just miserable," he said, "but I had to play it." (Stan and Marilyn Peterson; *Salt Lake Tribune*, 11/04/96)

PETERSON FAMILY

Rod Peterson knows every golf course in Utah!

TENNIS

LEILANI RORANI

Leilani Rorani was ranked the number one squash player in the world in 2002 while serving as a Primary teacher.

SQUASH CHAMPION—WOMEN. Leilani Marsh Rorani, Invercargill 1st Branch, Invercargill, New Zealand, became the best LDS women's squash player when she was ranked number one in the world, and went on to prove it (after healing from an injury that year) to win double gold medals for her home country of New Zealand at the 2002 Commonwealth Games in Manchester, England. She was competing against players from 72 other nations. Squash is similar to racquetball and is a very rigorous, tiring game. She and her husband, Blair, are the parents of a son, Joseph, and she serves in the Primary presidency of her home ward. (*Church News*, 3/27/04)

BEST TABLE TENNIS. Three generations of the Misbach family have dominated table tennis in Utah Valley and at other national events for several years, and in 2006, they finally competed together. At the Utah Valley Table Tennis Tournament held in Pleasant Grove, Utah, on April 22, 2006, all three generations were represented in the final rounds. Granddad Grant

MISBACH FAMILY

Misbach, 76, of the Edgemont 2nd Ward, Provo Utah Edgemont Stake, won first in his age group, while his son Matt (Canyon View 10th Ward, Orem Utah Canyon View Stake) was Grant's partner in men's doubles, taking second. Matt's son Colin (age 7) won 4th place for those 14 and under, while another of Grant's grandsons, Hayden Brown (age 7, of the Jacobs Ranch Ward, Saratoga Springs Utah Stake) took third place for those 14 and under. Back in 1955–57, Grant was the BYU champion in singles and doubles, and the rest has been a very fun history. "I've won more trophies than I can keep track of," Grant said. In 1976, he and his four boys (Brian, Greg, Alan, and Matt) won trophies at the Intermountain Table Tennis Tournament in Salt Lake City. "That was a very memorable experience," Grant says. Nowadays, he's in charge of the Huntsman Games table tennis competitions in Utah. (Grant Misbach, 5/6/06)

MISBACH FAMILY

Three generations of the Misbach family have excelled in table tennis at Utah and national tournaments.

STRENGTH—MEN

STRONGEST FATHER-SON POWERLIFTING TEAM. Champion powerlifter David Oyler and his son Michael, both members of the Schaumburg Illinois Stake, became the strongest father-son team in February 2004, after winning a national championship. They earned first place at the Natural Athletes Strength Association, where a strict drug-free training program is enforced.

This was the 14th time that David has won first place, and it's the second championship for Michael. In the process of winning, David also set new American and World Master class records for competitors age 40 and above. David lifted 716 pounds in the deep squat, 424 pounds in the bench press, and 640 pounds in the dead lift, for a total of 1,780 pounds. Michael curled 61 pounds, benched 115 pounds, and dead lifted 203 pounds to take first place in the youth division. (*Church News*, 3/13/04)

DAVID OYLER

David Oyler deep squats 716 pounds.

BENCH PRESS—AGE 20 AND UNDER, MEN. Blake Wright, Mt. Olympus 2nd, Mt. Olympus Stake, set a personal best before at age 20 by benching 405 pounds. (Author's interview, 8/27/05)

DAVID OYLER

Blake Wright benching 405 pounds.

FILE PHOTO

POWERLIFTING (2004 WORLD RECORD). In November 2004, Lance Davis of Lehi, Utah, set a new world record for the deadlift in the 259-pound class with an amazing floor to upright lift of 618.3 pounds, setting a new world record. The following June, he lifted 622.7 pounds. (Author's interview)

Lance Davis setting a new world record with a lift of 618.3 pounds in 2004.

BEST BENCH PRESS—MEN, 198-POUND CLASS (2005 WORLD RECORD). Eric Millburn, South Jordan, Utah, set a new world record for bench press in his weight class by lifting 534.5 pounds, shattering the previous world record by more than 50 pounds. (*South Valley Journal*, 1/06)

Eric Millburn set a new world record by lifting 534.5 pounds in 2005.

ERIC MILLBURN

BEST BENCH PRESS—SENIOR MEN. It's the same weight as many members' home storage supply of wheat, yet at age 71, Wilbert Kekahuna Kaimikaua, 71, Hoolehua Ward, Kahului Hawaii Stake, won the World Association of Bench Press and Dead Lifters Championship in November 2006 with a bench press of 374.5 pounds. Working his way through state and world competitions in 2006 was steady and sure, despite having had four open-heart surgeries during the prior years. "Healthy eating, physical activity and obedience to the Lord's commandments are my priorities," he told the *Church News*. (*Church News*, 1/20/07)

ROBERT GENT

Robert Gent pushes 885 pounds 18 inches away from his body using his legs.

LEG PRESS—MASTERS DIVISION (60–64 AGE). On September 30, 2001, Robert Gent of Beaver, Utah, put his 5-foot-eleven-inch and 175-pound frame behind 885 pounds and pushed in 18 inches away from his body. The Gold medal-winning leg press won Brother Gent a Gold Medal at the Las Vegas Athletic Club, Nevada Senior Olympics. (Robert R. Gent, 1/10/05)

BEST SENIOR ATHLETE (60–64), TRACK AND FIELD. Robert Gent, Beaver, Utah, may well be the most accomplished athlete for his age group in LDS men's track and field. He has more than 30 years of multi-event championships, and continues to up his endurance as the years pass. For example, for his 63rd birthday in 2004, he performed 63 repetitions of five events in about 63 seconds: 63 push-ups (in under 63 seconds); 63 leg squats (in 63 seconds); 63 crunches (in 65 seconds); 63 leg hops (in under 63 seconds); 63 dips (under 63 seconds). Maintaining his fitness required a change in diet, something

ROBERT GENT

Robert Gent's fitness includes a special diet he calls his "jet fuel" that includes 90 percent raw foods.

he calls his "jet fuel." A full 90 percent of everything Brother Gent eats is raw; the other 10 percent is steamed. There's no meat in there, only organic fruits, vegetables, herbs, grains, and water. Water is his choice of drink, and he drinks a lot. A former walk-on BYU track and field athlete, Gent has won numerous national Masters championships. In 2002 he won the North American Track and Field Championship (60–64 age) in the pentathlon (long jump, javelin, 200 meters, discus, 1500 meters). (Robert R. Gent, 1/10/05)

MOST PUSH-UPS, 1-MINUTE— BOYS, 16. On April 30, 2005, Brett Francis, West Point 12th Ward, West Point Utah Stake, did 99 push-ups in one minute at age 16. (Audrey J. Francis, 2/28/06)

AUDREY FRANCIS

Brett Francis

MOST SIT-UPS NONSTOP. Who has the record for the most sit-ups performed without stopping? Philip Snyder managed to do 1,100 sit-ups at one time during a meet in high school. His wife, Deborah, reports her husband was so intent on the record that he inadvertently rubbed his posterior side raw from the friction on the gym floor, something he didn't discover until he finished and went to shower. Ouch! (Deborah Snyder, 11/15/04)

STRENGTH—WOMEN

BEST WEIGHTLIFTER—YOUNG WOMEN, AGE 16–18. In July 2007, Michelle Glasgow, age 17 and a senior at Provo High in Utah, won the 2007 National School Age Championships in weightlifting, held in Springfield, Missouri. A few weeks later, she was officially notified of her selection to attend the Pan American Sub 17 Weightlifting Championships in Quebec. Michelle's

GLASGOW FAMILY

Michelle Glasgow is a typical 17-year-old, except for being a national champion!

events include the snatch where the lifter bends with the legs and in one motion lifts the bar from the platform to the full extend of the arms overhead. Her personal best in the snatch is 148 pounds. Her other event is the clean and jerk, where the weights are lifted to the shoulders and then, using legs and arms, raised overhead to the full extend of the arms. Her best in the clean and jerk is 200 pounds. She can also squat 250 pounds. (BYU NewsNet, 8/8/07; Scott Glasgow [Michelle's dad], 8/8/07)

STRONGEST FEMALE, 53-KILOGRAM (116.84 POUNDS) CLASS. For the second year in a row, Melanie Roach of the Bonney Lake Ward, Puyallup Washington Stake, won the 2007 National Weightlifting Championship in the 53-kilogram class. At

Melanie Roach wins the 2007 US weightlifting championship with a clean and jerk twice her own weight.

ROB MACKLEM

the Chicago, Illinois, meet she snatched 172 pounds and did a clean and jerk that was twice her body weight at 233.69 pounds. This was her seventh title overall. The win qualified her for the four-women Pan American Team that went to the Pan American Games in Rio de Janeiro, Brazil, in July, and she also earned a spot on the 2007 World Team that went to the World Championships in Thailand in September 2007. (*Church News*, 4/2/07)

ARM WRESTLING, WOMEN. In 2002, petite Nina Hansen of the Cedar City 6th Ward, Cedar Utah North Stake, who measures up at 126 pounds and 5 feet 5 inches tall, won the 2002 Women's World Arm Wrestling Championship (right arm) and was second place champion in the left arm. She has won numerous other local, national, and international competitions in arm wrestling, swimming, and other athletic events, and was one of two people named Athlete of the Year in 2002 for the Utah Summer Games.

Sister Hansen's arm wrestling strength comes from determination as much as training. "Boys were always challenging me to an arm wrestle," she told the *Cedar City Review*. When she was a freshman in high school at age 15, she was still quite the tomboy and showed up at a Church Gold and Green Ball held in Twin Falls, Idaho, in some denim jeans. Her father sent her home to change into something more feminine, namely a dress, and while she was gone a braggart high school senior boasted he could beat anybody in arm wrestling. Nina's dad said his daughter could beat him, and the two made

NINA HANSEN

Nina Hansen won the Women's World Arm Wrestling Championship in 2002 for right arm and took second with her left arm. A very talented mother of two, she also plays the cello and performed with the Chinese Hunan Symphony Orchestra.

a bet. The young man accepted. When Nina returned in her dress, the whole dance stopped to watch as they squared off at a table in the kitchen. "He outweighed me by 50 pounds," Nina said. "There we were, in front of all 500 people at the dance. We were pretty evenly matched but my endurance outdid his and I beat him." She said it was really fun!

But Nina is a tough fighter in other ways, having conquered Hodgkin's Disease, a form of cancer that had reached stage 4. "It was pretty bad," she said. They removed a football-sized tumor from her chest, and she fought the rest with chemo and radiation.

NINA HANSEN

Nina Hansen served a mission to Canada, and self-taught herself to play banjo, guitar, and French horn.

Sister Hansen is also a very accomplished cello player and traveled to China in 2006 to perform four concerts with the Hunan Symphony Orchestra. She said all the people were very kind and treated her like a celebrity. She's a returned missionary from the Canada Calgary Mission, and taught herself to play banjo, guitar, harmonica, French horn, and the hulusi (a Chinese gourd instrument). She's a competitive swimmer, and during her years at BYU, she was the catcher on the women's softball team and played for the Y's hockey team, both for four years. Today she lives in Cedar City, Utah, raising her two boys. "The most important things in my life," Sister Hansen says, "are my children, my Savior, my testimony, my health, my music and then my championships." (Gloria Darley, 2/25/05; *Cedar City Review*, 9/21/06; Author's interview, 10/5/07)

NINA HANSEN

Nina Hansen and her two sons

MOST STEPS, WOMEN. Who can claim the most steps counted for any duration of time or distance? For an exercise program, Susan Starkweather, Provo, Utah, kept a pedometer on her to track steps. At the end of a 90-day period in 2005, she finished off the program with 18,615 steps in one day, capping off a total of 734,329 steps. (Author's interview, 6/16/05)

RODEO/EQUESTRIAN/JOCKEY

BASCOM FAMILY

Earl W. Bascom in 1939.

MR. RODEO, EARL BASCOM. The Bascom family is as much a part of rodeo as Edison is the light bulb. Earl W. Bascom, the most well known of an outstanding and talented family, was central to bringing rodeo to the wide appeal and popularity it has today.

Dotted across the country are rodeos, halls of fame, bronco days, and celebrations all to honor this great man. His name is found in the United States Sports Academy, the Canadian Rodeo Hall of Fame, the Cowboy Memorial Museum in California, the Cowboy Rodeo Hall of Fame in California, and the Marion County Cattlemen's Hall of Fame in Mississippi, just to name a few. He was a Fellow of the Royal Society of Arts in London, England, and the oldest cowboy ever elected a member of the Professional Rodeo Cowboy Artist Association.

Brother Bascom brought two personal inventions to the sport that made all the difference. In 1922, he created the first hornless bronc saddle. On a bucking horse, a rider could slam into the horn and suffer serious injury, or it could snag his belt and throw the rider to the ground right in front of the horse. Two years later he introduced the one-hand bareback rigging that wraps around the horse with a single handle on the top for that famous one-handed rodeo ride. By the 1930s, Bascom's Rigging was the premier rigging to have and became professional rodeo's standard design.

Bascom competed in rodeo from 1916 to 1940 in the saddle bronc, bareback, bull riding, steer wrestling, and steer decorating. In 1933 he set a world speed record for steer decorating. He won the all-around championship title and also placed second in the North American Championship and third in the world. In 1940, after earning his way through college, he was named Rodeo's First Collegiate Cowboy. And still standing today in Mississippi is the first permanent rodeo arena and grandstands that he designed and supervised.

Bascom's list of lasting achievements is legendary. He

FILE PHOTO

Three amigos. Turk Greenough, Roy Rogers, and Earl Bascom partner up to talk over old times.

worked on some of the largest ranches in Canada and the U.S. He broke and raised hundreds of horses, and chased wild horses in the badlands of Utah, Colorado, Wyoming, Montana, and Canada. He worked cattle drives and was acquainted with lawmen and outlaws, Indians and Indian fighters, gunslingers, squatters, and homesteaders.

Earl Bascom was born in Vernal, Utah, and was one of 11 children. The family moved to Alberta, Canada, where a fascination with rodeo kept Earl and his brothers busy making up their own rodeos. "We got a lot of practice riding anything that walked, crawled, or bucked," he said. As an adult, he was an experienced bronc buster, cowpuncher, trail driver, blacksmith, freighter, stagecoach driver, miner, trapper, wolf hunter, wild horse chaser, rancher, and dude wrangler. He was also a Hollywood movie actor right alongside Roy Rogers.

BASCOM FAMILY

John W. Bascom, Raymond, Earl, Mel, and Weldon, 1939.

The "Bascom Boys" included Earl and his brothers Raymond, Melvin, and Weldon. In 1916, they designed and built the world's first side-delivery rodeo chute. And with their dad's help (John W. Bascom), they built rodeo's first reverse opening rodeo chute.

In his later years, Brother Bascom painted and sculpted bronze rodeo activities and became world famous for his artwork. He also served as bishop and stake patriarch in the Victorville California Stake. In 1995 this bright-eyed, alert, and congenial 89-year-old champion finally gathered up his memories and experiences for the last time, and carried the world's last link to the old West out across the range to a place of greener pastures. "If you want to be a champion bull rider," he often said, "you have to ride the toughest bull." (John Bascom [son of Earl] and the numerous articles he provided, 2006)

Earl Bascom's talent as a sculptor and painter is world renowned with some of his pieces adorning the display cases of presidents and museums.

FILE PHOTO

FILE PHOTO

Texas Rose Bascom

QUEEN OF RODEO. Texas Rose Bascom, part Cherokee and Choctaw Indian, was a professional trick roper, trick rider, and movie actress known worldwide as Queen of the Trick Ropers. She married Weldon Bascom of the famous Bascom Boys, and learned to rope and ride from the well-known cowgirl Pearl Elder. She won worldwide acclaim for her rodeo, stage, and movie performances. During the 1940s she joined USO and toured with Bob Hope, Roy Rogers, Dale Evans, Gabby Hayes, Hoot Gibson, and Monty Montana. "They were the sons of the pioneers," she said. She was selected to be the U.S. representative at the International Folk Festival, performed at the Hollywood Bowl, and rode in the Pasadena Rose Parade. She performed in several Hollywood movies and was the first Latter-day Saint inducted into the National Cowgirl Hall of Fame. (John Bascom, 2006)

Texas Rose Bascom was known as the Queen of Trick Ropers and performed with Bob Hope, among others. She was billed as "the most beautiful stage performer in the world."

RACING HORSES. There have been a number of excellent horses bred for the track, and as those horses and their LDS owners make themselves known, we'll begin a listing here. To date we have two entries:

Swaps, Kentucky Derby Winner. Easily the world's best horse during his prime, and possibly the best horse to put hoof to turf, Swaps was the cover story for magazines around the country in 1955–56. The National Museum of Racing and Hall of Fame reports Swaps set five world records at a mile or more, three track records, equaled an American turf record, and won the Kentucky Derby, San Vicente, Santa Anita Derby, Will Rogers, Californian, and the American Derby. Swaps was named

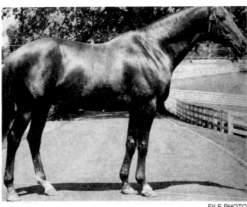

Rex Ellsworth told folks he treated Swaps like a horse, not a pet dog as the eastern Kentucky horse breeders did—much to their dismay!

Horse of the Year at age 4 in 1956, and won the Argonaut, Inglewood, American, Hollywood Gold Cup, Sunset, and Washington Park Handicaps.

MARK KILLIAN

Swaps genealogy takes him back through War Admiral and Iron Reward to the immortal Man O' War. He produced some champions, too: Chateaugay, who won the 1963 Kentucky Derby and Belmont Stakes; and Queen of Queens, a Hall of Fame filly ranked 81st in the list of greatest race horses ever. Swaps is ranked 20th, but many believe the rank too low. In all, Swaps produced 35 stakes winners from his 425 foals.

Brother Rex Ellsworth and family raised Swaps to be one of the best racing horses ever. They sold him for $2 million, plus options.

He earned his LDS owners $848,900 in three years of racing and $3 million as a sire. Swaps was inducted into the Hall of Fame in 1966 and died in 1972 at age 20. (Author's interview with Mark Killian, 6/8/07; www.racingmuseum.org)

Brother Derek. A shiny bay colt who became the betting favorite across America in 2006 was named for an LDS missionary who was serving in Armenia at the time: Elder Derek Tillotson. In the horse-trading business nowadays, it works like this: Elder Tillotson's dad and a partner buy yearlings at auction. The men train the horses and sell them the following year as two-year-olds in training. The yearlings are unnamed when they're bought, but within a year, they must have a name. Brother Tillotson's partner, a Catholic, does the buying of the yearlings and was so impressed with the young missionary son of his partner that he named the horse after him, Brother Derek. The horse cost $150,000, and after gliding through a quarter mile in less than 21 seconds, he was sold for $275,000. By the time Brother Derek tied for fourth in 2006 at his first Kentucky Derby, he had won purse money totaling $1,162,080. (*Deseret News*, 3/7/06, 5/6–7/06)

RODEO CHAMP (2007 WORLD CHAMPION). Matt Sherwood, Pima 2nd Ward, Pima Arizona Stake, won the National Finals Rodeo as team roping header on December 9, 2006. The competition, held in Las Vegas, Nevada, brought together the 15 top contestants in team roping and seven other rodeo events to sort out the best of the best. Brother Sherwood, 37, was invited along with 14 others based on money won so far that year. He had an $8,000 lead from wins in other rodeo events across the country. Sherwood's participation in professional rodeo started in 1994, but he didn't go full time until 2006, when he sold his tile and flooring company in Queen Creek, Arizona, and hit the trail. Sherwood and his wife, Kim, are parents of seven children. (*Church News*, 1/27/07; ESPN)

ARCHERY

BEST ARCHER (2001 WORLD RECORD). On February 6, 2001, Roger Hoyle, Cedar City 2nd Ward, Cedar City Utah West Stake, set a new world record for outdoor compound-bow target shooting with a score of 1414 at the U.S. Team Trials for the World Championships in Flushing, New York. This beat the old world record of 1409, and the elusive target in this sport is the perfect 1440. Brother Hoyle made the U.S. team for that year but didn't compete because of travel restrictions resulting from the 9/11 terror attacks. (Roger Hoyle, 12/11/04)

BOWLING

ALLEN FAMILY

Maude Porter Allen

OLDEST BOWLER. Maude Porter Allen, Ogden, Utah, saw a lot of life until she began to lose her eyesight in her 90s. Among her other adventures such as a mission with her husband in 1952, she was one of about 30 children from a polygamous family forced to flee when Pancho Villa's rebels forced the Saints out of Mexico in 1912. But that failing eyesight was particularly frustrating because it was wrecking her game—her passion for bowling. With one eye blind and barely able to see in the other, she still bowled three games, twice a week, against her sister Mabel Carroll, until just after her 99th birthday. And she was pretty good, too, averaging more than 100 points a game. (Lee Ann Partington, great-granddaughter who bowled with Maude after her 99th birthday; 1/27/04)

JEFF VIOLA

PERFECT BOWLER. Members of the Church who have achieved that glorious and exalted place of perfection by bowling 12 straight strikes for a 300 begins with Jeff Viola of Bowling Green, Ohio, who bowled a perfect 300 on July 12, 1983, at age 22. His brother Doug also bowled a 300, making them the first LDS brothers to bowl the perfect game. (Jeff Viola, 11/21/04)

Is Jeff Viola the first Latter-day Saint to bowl a perfect 300? All perfect bowlers are invited to contact the author for consideration for the next edition of *Mormon World Records*. See www.mormonworldrecords.com.

AUTOMOTIVE/MOTORCYCLES

FASTEST DRIVE DOWN CANADA, NORTH-SOUTH (1994 WORLD RECORD). On September 19, 1994, Stephen Harvey, Brockville Branch, Kingston Ontario Canada District, began an amazing trek from the uppermost realms of the Canadian wastelands to its most southern point at Pt. Pelee, Ontario. Stephen was joined by his brother, Will Harvey of the Fayetteville Ward, Arkansas, and father William Harvey of Burlington Ward, Hamilton Ontario Canada, for the 4,700-mile trek that took a record time of 83 hours 19 minutes.

STEVE HARVEY

Getting started. The Harveys cross the Arctic Circle at latitude 66° 33′ north, on Dempster Highway, a road of shale and limestone built three feet above the tundra.

The adventure had some interesting challenges. Guinness World Records won't participate in anything illegal, so the Harveys had to maintain a speed anticipated by vehicles traveling at the posted speed limits. Also, what car to drive? Ford was debuting its new Contour with a V-tech engine, so a prototype was donated, with specially fitted mud flaps. They equipped themselves with an onboard fridge, CB radio, cell phones, a laptop, and an extensive first aid kit.

They were flown to Whitehorse, where they picked up the car and drove 1,200 miles to Inuvik in the Northwest Territories. At 9 AM on September 19, 1994, the family sped off (at the speed limit!) down an amazing patch of civilization called Dempster Highway. This highway cuts across the frozen tundra that is an otherwise impassible, spongy surface for which wheeled vehicle travel is virtually impossible.

The highway is a single-lane grade of gravel and limestone that is three-feet thick. Ford Canada provided an extra windshield in case flying rock caused problems. For those 10 hours, the constant roar of rocks pounding the bottom of the vehicle was almost deafening. Coming around a bend, they suddenly came upon a herd of 10–15 horses and slammed on the brakes.

STEVE HARVEY

Crossing into the Northwest Territory—in September!

171

STEVEN HARVEY

The car slid to within six inches of a horse's rear end. Had they hit, the horse could have hoofed trip-ending damage. They also encountered blizzards and high snow drifts with glass-smooth ice that hampered progress.

The shifts were four hours each: to sleep, drive, and navigate. If the excitement kept any of them awake during their sleeping time, that was too bad; the rotating shifts had to continue. Gas station breaks included precision timing as gas flowed, trips were made to the bathroom, and jumping jacks were done to put blood back into tired limbs. They made 13 gas stops. When they finally pulled into Pt. Pelee, Ontario, a part of Canada that is farther South than Washington and North Dakota, they were met by four major television stations and major newspapers, and the human interest element pushed more sobering news off the front pages all across Canada. In total, they gave about 40 interviews.

After a week of nonstop driving on an assortment of roads, having visited the mayors of Leamington and Inuvik, and having enjoyed among other things a Caribou steak and a Musk Ox burger, the Harveys celebrated (alcohol free, of course!) the conclusion of a once-in-a-lifetime trip down the vast beautiful scenery of north-to-south Canada. They set a new world record for the fastest drive across Canada from north to south, ending their adventure in Ontario.

"The hardest part of the trip," Stephen said, "was not sleeping when it was my turn. The best part was being with my dad and brother, and enjoying that incredible scenery and Northern lights." (Stephen Harvey, 10/18/04)

WORLDWIDE WORLD RECORDS

Since the 2004 premier edition of *The Skousen Book of Mormon World Records*, numerous new friends from around the world have contacted the author with personal achievements that are extraordinary and fantastic. Expanding this collection to include these new friends of other faiths, or none at all, creates a new opportunity to learn from the powerful example and inspirational achievements of others that can motivate, encourage, and promote the best out of each of us. The author is honored and proud to include the following records submitted by one of these newfound friends in this special new section, "Worldwide World Records."

MOST WORLD RECORDS—ENDURANCE. Paddy Doyle was born in 1964 in Birmingham, England. By the age of eight he had learned judo, and by 11 he was an excellent boxer for his age. But growing up on the streets of Birmingham was a rough beginning for many youth in those days, and Paddy was frequently in trouble for picking fights and getting in trouble with the law. During those growing-up years, he seemed to attract trouble and thought himself on a path destined for a life in and out of prison. That's when a copy of the *Guinness Book of World Records* landed in his life, and suddenly he had a positive direction for his youthful passions. He decided he wanted to be the best in the world—in something. And that something grew into dozens as his hard work, talents, and abilities lofted him to become the best in the world in literally dozens of athletic records.

PADDY DOYLE

Paddy Doyle holds the world record for the most one arm (top) and back of hands push-ups (bottom).

Paddy Doyle's autobiography tells of a young boy on his way to self-destruction when the promise of athletic achievement knocked on his door.

Today, Paddy lives in Sheldon, near Birmingham, and runs numerous personal safety and martial arts courses. On the walls of his home and offices, in drawers and in scrapbooks, are certificates and letters affirming his position as

PADDY DOYLE

Paddy Doyle's endurance on various weight machines is unmatched in several categories.

the world's best from decades past right up to today in physical feats that are fantastic to contemplate and exhausting to challenge.

As of this writing, Paddy has been in the *Guinness Book of World Records* about 40 times and has achieved 156 fitness endurance records for strength, speed, and stamina. One of his most amazing records is more than 1.5 million push-ups in one year. Listed below are Paddy's records and the dates he achieved them.

For more information about this amazing man and great friend of this author, see www.worldsfittestathlete.co.uk to order his delightful autobiography *Iron Man* or *Record Breaker*.

World Record **NR**=National Record **ER**=European Record **BR**=British Record
CR=Course Record **MR**=British Military Record
RR=Regional Record

#	Date	Event	Duration	New Record	Venue	Record
1	28.05.87	Push-ups 50-lb plate	4 hrs 30 mins	4,100	Germany	WR
2	01.05.88	13 mile 43-lb backpack half marathon	1 hr 59 mins		UK	ER
3	28.08.88	Sit-ups 50-lb plate	5 hrs	5,000	UK	WR
4	21.10.88 –1.10.89	Push-ups in a year	12 months	1,500,230	UK	WR
5	01.05.89	Push-ups in 24 hrs	24 hrs	37,350	UK	ER
6	18.04.90	Samson's chair		4 hrs 40 mins	UK	ER
7	06.05.90	One-arm push-ups	10 mins	400	UK	BR
8	20.05.90	Squat thrusts in 1 hr	1 hr	2,275	UK	ER
9	31.07.90	Push-ups one arm	5 hrs	7,643	UK	ER
10	26.09.90	Sit-ups 50-lb plate	15 mins	376	UK	NR
11	09.11.90	Weight lifting in 1 hr	1 hr	53,480 lbs	UK	RR
12	09.11.90	110-lb coal bag (25 meters)	1 hr	149	UK	RR

Paddy Doyle set the world records for the most sparing rounds in a year, a week, and the most 1-minute rounds without stopping.

PADDY DOYLE

#	Date	Event	Duration	New Record	Venue	Record
13	22.02.91	World Speed Versatility	45 mins		UK	WR
		a) Sit-ups 50-lb plate	5 mins	117		
		b) Squats	5 mins	260		
		c) Squat thrusts	5 mins	340		
		d) Weight lifting 9,000 lbs	1 min 40 secs			
		e) 400 meter 40-lb backpack run	2 mins 58 secs			
		f) 800 meter 40-lb backpack run	2 mins 30 secs			
		g) 200 meter 116-lb coal bag	4 mins 20 secs			
		h) 400 meter 116-lb coal bag Finishing time 33 mins. Athlete to complete all events to claim record.	33 mins			WR
14	07.03.91	Sit-ups 50-lb plate	30 mins	580	UK	NR
15	21.04.91	44-lb backpack marathon		4 hrs 42 mins	UK	WR
16	03.08.91	Sit-ups 50-lb plate	5 mins	152	UK	RR
17	03.08.91	Sit-ups 50-lb plate	10 mins	292	UK	RR
18	03.08.91	Sit-ups 50-lb plate	15 mins	427	UK	RR
19	19.09.91	1/2 mile 40-lb backpack treadmill (indoor)	2 mins 58 secs		UK	WR
20	07.12.91	5 mile 40-lb backpack treadmill (indoor)	37 mins 45 secs		UK	WR
21	07.12.91	1 mile 40-lb backpack (indoor)		6 mins 8 secs	UK	ER

PADDY DOYLE

PADDY DOYLE

Step-ups with a weight is a grueling event that simulates an up- and down-hill climb at the same time.

Paddy Doyle often takes to the outdoors for climbs with a weighted backpack to train military and other groups in endurance events and competitions.

#	Date	Event	Duration	New Record	Venue	Record
22	19.02.92	Burpees (indoor)	15 mins	470	UK	ER
23	19.02.92	Burpees (indoor)	30 mins	860	UK	ER
24	12.04.92	26 mile 365 yds 50-lb backpack marathon		5 hrs 4 mins	UK	WR
25	27.07.92	116-lb coal bag (25 meter) shuttle run		31 mins 32 secs	UK	WR
26	03.09.92	Squat thrusts alternate	1 hr	2,504	UK	ER
27	03.09.92	Squat thrusts alternate	30 mins	1,420	UK	ER
28	17.10.92	Sit-ups 50-lb plate	1 hr	1,193	UK	WR
29	06.02.93	Burpees (indoor)	1 hr	1,822	UK	ER
30	07.03.93	10 mile 40-lb backpack run		1 hr 24 mins	Ireland	WR
31	07.03.93	1 mile 40-lb backpack run		5 mins 35 secs	Ireland	WR
32	04.05.98	Squat thrusts	30 mins	1,871	UK	ER
33	15.05.88	43-lb backpack run (13miles)		2 hrs 9 mins	UK	BR
34	22.05.88	44-lb backpack run		4 hrs 56 mins	UK	ER
35	02.09.89	Squat thrusts	1 hr	2,010	UK	ER
36	12.11.89	Sit-ups 50-lb plate	1 hr	1,130	UK	ER
37	23.02.90	Squat thrusts	1 hr	2,150	UK	ER
38	06.05.90	One-arm push-ups	5 hrs	5,260	UK	ER
39	21.06.91	Burpees	1 hr	1,619	UK	BR

#	Date	Event	Duration	New Record	Venue	Record
40	14.09.91	1 mile backpack run		6 mins 56 secs	UK	ER
41	19.02.92	Burpees	1 hr	1,649	UK	ER
42	13.06.92	Squat thrusts alternative	30 mins	1,360	UK	BR
43	22.02.93	Burpees	15 mins	490	UK	WR
44	22.02.93	Burpees	30 mins	930	UK	WR
45	22.06.93	Push-ups	1 hr	1,705	UK	RR
46	01.08.93	Squat thrusts alternative	15 mins	745	UK	ER
47	06.08.93	Squat thrusts alternative	5 mins	290	UK	WR
48	06.08.93	Squat thrusts alternative	10 mins	545	UK	ER
49	04.09.93	40-lb backpack run (50 miles)		11:56:22.00	Ireland	WR
50	04.09.93	40-lb backpack run (42 miles)		9:57:22.00	Ireland	WR
51	27.11.93	One-arm push-ups	1 hr	1,886	UK	ER
52	06.02.94	Burpees	1 hr	1,840	UK	ER
53	06.02.94	Burpees	30 mins	920	UK	ER
54	06.02.94	Burpees	15 mins	475	UK	ER
55	15.02.94	Yearly boxing sparring record		4,006 rounds	UK	WR
56	10.04.94	4 speed records	1 hr		UK	WR
		One-arm push-ups	15 mins	429		
		Burpees	15 mins	323		
		Squat thrusts	15 mins	400		
		Alternative squat thrusts	15 mins	592		
57	23.05.94	Weekly boxing sparring record (3-min rounds)		183 rounds	UK	BR
58	24.06.94	One-arm push-ups	30 mins	1,000	UK	NR
59	29.07.94	Squat thrusts alternative	10 mins	574	UK	WR
60	19.08.94	Squat thrusts alternative	1 hr	2,810	UK	WR
61	19.08.94	Squat thrusts alternative	15 mins	790	UK	WR

Fitness events that include rowing are usually done in a gym instead of on a river or lake to reduce the variables involved and make the effort more comparable among athletes. Shown here, Paddy Doyle is at work on a rowing machine to challenge a world record in 2002.

PADDY DOYLE

#	Date	Event	Duration	New Record	Venue	Record
62	19.08.94	Squat thrusts alternative	30 mins	1,580	UK	WR
63	03.09.94	65-mile speed march weight carrying 30-lb backpack and 9-lb weight		24 hrs 55 mins	Ireland	ER
64	31.10.94	Endurance 56-lb log carrying		21 mins 40 secs	UK	WR
65	31.01.95 –6.02.95	Weekly full-contact middleweight sparring title		7 days 203 rounds	UK	NR
66	10.03.95	Worcester 2-mile run carrying 40-lb backpack		16 mins	UK	BR
67	22.04.95	5k 40-lb backpack run	25 mins 15 secs		Ireland	ER
68	22.04.95	4-1/4 miles backpack run carrying 40-lb backpack	34 min 54.2 secs		Ireland	WR
69	10.08.94	58-lb backpack run (5k)		32 mins 15 secs	Ireland	ER
70	27.05.95	Squat thrusts alternative	2 hrs	4,901	UK	WR
71	27.05.95	Squat thrusts alternative	1 hr	2,820	UK	WR
72	24.06.95	40-lb backpack multi-terrain course (15 miles)		2 hrs 35 mins	UK	ER
73	24.06.95	40-lb backpack multi-terrain course (25 miles)		5 hrs 45 mins	UK	ER
74	24.06.95	40-lb backpack multi-terrain course (30 miles)		7 hrs 15 mins	UK	ER

#	Date	Event	Duration	New Record	Venue	Record
75	12.08.95	Squat thrusts	2 hrs	3,597	UK	RR
76	12.08.95	Squat thrusts	30 mins	1,360	UK	RR
77	21.08.95	Full-contact fighters	1 month		UK	ER
		middleweight combat			UK	
		560 full contact middleweight combat rounds				
78	31.07.90	One-arm push-ups	30 mins	1,328	UK	
79	12.02.96	One-arm push-ups	1 hr	2,521	UK	WR
80	31.07.90	One-arm push-ups	1 hr	2,490	UK	WR
81	31.07.90	One-arm push-ups	2 hrs 30 mins	4,708	UK	WR
82	18.02.96	One-arm push-ups	7 days	16,723	UK	ER
83	25.11.95	Burpees circuit training	5 hrs	4,921	UK	WR
84	25.02.89	Consecutive push-ups	37 mins	1,740	UK	ER
85	25.02.89	Consecutive push-ups	3 hrs 54 mins	7,860	UK	ER
86	12.02.96	One-arm push-ups	5 hrs	8,794	UK	WR
87	26.07.96	26-mile endurance backpack run	6 hrs 28 mins	UK	WR	
88	23.09.96	WUMA freestyle sparring title	23 days	467 rounds	UK	NR
89	12.04.97	25-mile multi-terrain challenge carrying 40-lb backpack		6 hrs 55 mins	UK	WR
90	01.06.97	WUMA full-contact British title (10 days) challenge record	251 rounds		UKB	UK
91	09.08.97	28-mile multi-terrain challenge (40-lb backpack)		11 hrs 59 mins	UKB	UK
92	25.11.95	Burpees	1 hr	1,850	UK	WR
93	10-11.02	Weight distance carrying record			UK	ER
		20-lb backpack 9-lb 9-oz weight (77 mi 350 yds)			UK	
94	04.05.98	Squat thrusts	1 hr	3,743	UK	
95	10.05.98	Squat thrusts	7 days	21,347	UK	ER

#	Date	Event	Duration	New Record	Venue	Record
96	20.09.98	13-mile half marathon 40-lb backpack		1:58:24.00	UK	ER
97	09.05.99	56-lb backpack run (5 mile)		36 mins 49 secs	UK	WR
98	25.07.99	Circuit training (burpees) over 7 days	3 hrs per day	21,409	UK	NR
99	05.03.00	Back-of-hands push-ups	1 hr	660	UK	ER
100	06.05.00	Warlords Kumite world title	5 hours	131 rounds	UK	WR
101	07.07.00	Back of hands push-ups	30 mins	425	Germany	BR
102	22.08.00	Squat thrusts alternative	5 hrs	6,696	UK	NR
103	30.09.00	Martial arts boxing punch kick record	2 hrs	2,777 kicks 3,680 punches	UK	WR
104	11.03.01	Back of hands push-ups	15 mins	400	UK	BR
105	11.03.01	Back of hands push-ups	30 mins	689	UK	BR
106	21.03.01	Back of hands push-ups	1 hr	1,303	UK	ER
107	21.02.01	Back of hands push-ups	30 mins	700	UK	WR
108	24.06.01	Back of hands push-ups	1 min	70	UK	BR
109	27.02.99	British Challenge Boxing Martial Arts title record, 2-min rounds	14 days	292	UK	ER
110	30.09.00	Martial arts boxing Punch-kick record	1 hr	2,885 punches 1,995 kicks	UK	WR
111	09.05.99	6-mile run 56-lb backpack		53 mins 45 secs	UK	WR
112	19.08.01	Martial arts boxing Punch-kick record	1 hr	4,104 punches 1,560 kicks	UK	WR
113	15.06.96	RTE television Dublin 40-lb backpack run, on treadmill	50 mins	5.14 miles	UK	WR

#	Date	Event	Duration	New Record	Venue	Record
114	25.11.01	World speed challenge	58.42 secs	10 events	UK	WR
115	09.06.02	World kumite boxing title	3 hrs 8 mins	110 rounds	UK	WR
		title round				UK
116	11.08.02	Mount Snowdon special forces challenge 45-lb backpack - 1085 meters	3 hrs 20 mins	UK	CR	
117	25.09.02	World speed fitness challenge	12 mins		UK	WR
		Push-ups		123		
		Sit-ups		108		
		One-arm push-ups		114		
		Squat thrusts		90		
		Burpees		33		
		Back of hand push-ups		102		
118	28.09.02	Cotswold hill challenge carrying 40-lb backpack (25 mile)		8 hrs 34 mins	UK	CR
119	17.10.02	Versa stair climber carrying 40-lb backpack	1 hour	3144 ft	UK	ER
120	15.11.02	Versa stair climber carrying 40-lb backpack	30 mins	1696 ft	UK	BR
121	26.04.03	Special forces speed march challenge carrying 55-lb backpack (60 km/40 miles)		14 hrs 50 mins	UK	MR
122	1993-02	Most boxing martial arts rounds, 1993–2002; welter weight, middle weight, super middle weight	6,072	UK	WR	
123	07.12.02	SAS 25 km endurance march carrying 65-lb backpack		9 hrs 20 mins	UK	CR
124	08.11.03	World fittest man speed march challenge carrying 45-lb backpack (25 km)		8 hrs 10 mins	UK	CR

#	Date	Event	Duration	New Record	Venue	Record
125	14–15.04.04	12 fitness challenges		21:21:02.00	UK	WR
		12-mile walk				
		12-mile run				
		2-mile swim				
		110-mile cycle				
		312,170 lbs weight lift				
		1,250 push-ups				
		1,250 star jumps				
		3,250 sit-up crunches				
		20,000 meters rower				
		1,250 hip flexor reps 5-lb weight				
		1-mile run carrying 44-lb backpack				
		3 kilometers on gym stepper				
126	19.07.95	most para jumps in 1 minute	1 min	45	UK	WR
127	14.04.04	weight lifting free weights and machine weights Solihull, UK	1 hr	149,220 lb	UK	WR
128	6–7.11.04	World speed fitness record		13:59:55.00	Germany	WR
		1,750 meters swimming				
		20 km running				
		20 mile cycle				
		2,000 star jumps				
		2,000 sit ups				
		Weightlifting 141,150 kg,				
		1,400 machine hip flexors, 5-kg attached				
		2,326 meters carrying 40-lb backpack				

#	Date	Event	Duration	New Record	Venue	Record
		10,000 meters rowing				
		3 km stepper				
		500 alternative squat thrusts				
129	07.11.04	Full contact martial arts kicks	1 hr	2,805	Germany	WR
130	16.02.05	11 fitness challenges		18:56:09.00	UK	WR
		12 mile run				
		12 mile walk				
		1,250 push-ups				
		1,250 star jumps				
		3,250 sit-up crunches				
		1,250 standing hip flexors				
		110 mile cycle				
		20 mile rowing				
		20 mile cross trainer				
		Weightlifting, lift 300,000 lbs				
		2 mile swim				
131	13.08.05	World, 1 hour speed fitness record	1 hr		Germany	WR
		Rowing		2,070 meters		
		Cycling		5.8 km		
		Run with 40-lb backpack		1.29 km		
		Step versaclimber with 40-lb backpack	1,008			
		Weights—dumbbells		5,520 kg		
		Boxing punches		2,230		
132	13.08.05	World 1-minute punch record	1 min	470 punches	Germany	ER
133	19.11.05	WUMA warlords kumite title record	141 rounds		UK	WR
		Fought 141 one-minute rounds		117 wins, 24 losses		
134	15.02.93 –7.12.05	Most boxing martial arts fought		6264 rounds	UK	WR

#	Date	Event	Duration	New Record	Venue	Record
135	27.02.06	world fitness champions title record		17:12:33.00	UK	WR
		2 mile + 21 meter swim				
		20 mile row				
		20-1/4 mile cross trainer				
		10 mile speed march				
		100-1/4 mile cycle				
		550 star jumps				
		3,010 sit-up crunches				
		300,000-lb weight lifting				
		10-1/4 mile run				
		505 hanging leg lifts				
136	02.07.06	Sit-ups 50-lb weight on chest	5 mins	211	UK	WR
137	02.07.06	Sit-ups 50-lb weight on chest	10 mins	351	UK	WR
138	02.07.06	Sit-ups 50-lb weight on chest	15 mins	501	UK	WR
139	02.07.06	Sit-ups 50-lb weight on chest	30 mins	932	UK	WR
140	16.04.99	Most back of hands push-ups	5 mins	327	UK	WR
141	05.08.06	World ultra fitness challenge			USA	WR
		Treadmill run with 40-lb backpack 1 hour	5.05 miles			
		Shuttle sprints (30 feet) with 40-lb backpack	1 hour	512 sprints		
		Standing chest press with 30-lb weight	1 hour	713 reps		
		Step-ups carrying 40-lb backpack	1 hour	835 steps		
		Cycle	1 hour	21.6 miles		

#	Date	Event	Duration	New Record	Venue	Record
142	09.11.06	step-ups carrying 56-lb backpack	1 hour	716 step-ups	UK	WR
143	19.01.07	Most full contact martial arts strikes	1 hour	18,372	UK	WR
144	19.01.07	Most boxing full contact upper body	1 minute	586	UK	WR
145	24.02.07	Cross country marathon carrying 40-lb backpack	9:08:00.00	26 miles	UK	CR
146	18.04.07	World speed challenge record	1 hour	14 records	USA	WR
147	20.04.07	Step-ups carrying 40-lb backpack on 15-in. bench	1 hour	911 step-ups	USA	WR
148	07.07.07	Cross country marathon carrying 45-lb backpack		7:37:02.00	UK	CR
149	08.11.07	Training squats	1 hour	4,708	UK	WR
150	08.11.07	Martial arts kicks	1 hour	5.570	UK	WR
151	08.11.07	Back of hand push-ups	15 min.	672	UK	WR
152	08.11.07	Back of hand push-ups	30 min.	1,387	UK	WR
153	08.11.07	Back of hand push-ups	1 hour	1,904	UK	WR
154	08.11.07	World fitness strength record (in 7 hours)			UK	WR

10 mile speed marching carrying 56-lb backpack

63 mile cycling

367 back of hands push-ups

633 squats

830 full contact martial arts kicks

PADDY DOYLE

PADDY DOYLE

Above: Back-of-hands push-ups test a person's arm and body strength as well as his or her ability to endure pain. In 2007, Paddy did 1,386 such push-ups in 30 minutes, setting a new world record.

Above: Step-ups with an extra 40 pounds simulates climbing a hill with a backpack, something for which the military trains. In 2007, Paddy made 911 step-ups in one hour using a 15-inch bench. It was a new world record.

Right: Paddy Doyle and trainer John Williams hold an edition of *Guinness World Records* in which Paddy has several world records. Since this photo was taken, he has added several more world records and continues to improve on that even today.

PADDY DOYLE

PADDY DOYLE

Paddy holds the world record for the most martial arts kicks at 5,750 in one hour (left). He also holds the world record for the most circuit training squats at 4,708 in 1 hour (right). The squat exercise works every muscle in the body . . . and for the rest of us who try it, the difficulty becomes pretty obvious after 5 minutes! But Paddy just keeps going and going.

PADDY DOYLE

INDEX

C

INDEX BY CHURCH UNIT
OR LOCATION

ABOUT THE AUTHOR

PAUL B. SKOUSEN

Fred Morrison (that young man on the right), inventor of the Frisbee, can still make a power throw with the best of them at age 87.

Paul B. Skousen has been slaughtering the English language for 30 years at firms and agencies in New York; Washington, D.C.; and downtown Lindon, Utah. His writings have confused corporate executives, senators, congressmen, the CIA, the FBI, Ronald Reagan, and George Bush, Sr.—but usually in a good way. He also speaks fluent three-year-old.

He invented a mathematical formula to get something for nothing, published a joke in *Reader's Digest*, drove a semi-trailer truck in circles, and delivered two babies on purpose.

He holds the record for the longest paper-airplane flight in a BYU ballroom, he built a solar bread baker, he set a 100-yard-dash record in high school, he built a model sailing ship from scratch, he played the tenor sax in Reno, he made roof trusses by hand, he started a rumor that was published in *Time* magazine, he asked Gerald Ford two loaded questions, he enjoyed a first-name friendship with Ollie North, and he was the subject of Paul Harvey's "The Rest of the Story." He once broke his dog's tail.

He has stood between the paws of the Sphinx, crept inside the Great Pyramids, swam in the Dead Sea, climbed the hill of Calvary, caught Pharaoh's Revenge in Jordan, excavated ancient pottery, snorkeled in the Caribbean, toured a loaded missile silo, stepped in poo outside of Luxor, walked right past Toronto's Hockey Hall of Fame, got sunburned in Maui, changed the orbit of a spy satellite, held counterfeit $100 bills, mortally wounded a yapping dog in Belgium, got seasick in St. Thomas, test-fired a captured AK-47, got lost in the belly of a spy

PAUL B. SKOUSEN

Presidential candidate Ron Paul stops by for some advice. (Yeah, right.)

PAUL B. SKOUSEN

Jordan's former Prime Minster Majali stops by for some advice. (Yeah, right.)

PAUL B. SKOUSEN

World's best fisherman, Ray Johnson, stops by for some advice. (Yeah, right.)

plane, wailed at the Wailing Wall, jay-walked in Rome, watched a midnight storm at Nagshead, yelled at a drug smuggler in Tijuana, smelled $50 million in used cash, changed a diaper atop the World Trade Center, passed a kidney stone, was stung raising honey bees, flew in the President's seat aboard Marine One, ate fondue in Lucerne, peeled off a piece of foil from Apollo 11, climbed inside a smuggled Soviet MiG 21, got caught smooching in Parley's Canyon, confessed to it on live radio, and witnessed his wife writing the first check at the new Nauvoo Temple clothing desk. He once measured the speed of light.

PAUL B. SKOUSEN

Touching the wall. Israel's security fence includes many miles of movable 25-foot tall cement panels. How good is it? Terror attacks have been reduced by more than 97 percent since its installation.

He has shoveled the walks for President Ezra Taft Benson, collected fast offerings from Marvin J. Ashton, and shook the hands of President David O. McKay, Harold B. Lee, Spencer W. Kimball, Ezra T. Benson, Gordon B. Hinckley, Thomas M. Monson, and Miss Universe 1984. However, none will admit this.

He and his wife, Kathy Bradshaw Skousen, are the parents of 10 children—all boys except for six girls. For genealogical purposes, she is his fourth cousin twice removed. He was educated at BYU and Georgetown University, has published the premier edition of *Mormon World Records* and *Brother Paul's Mormon Bathroom Reader*, and is a high priest doing whatever the bishop asks of him in his Alpine 5th Ward, Alpine Utah West Stake. No hobbies.

PAUL B. SKOUSEN

The whole gang in 2007. Bottom (l-r): Maryann, Julie, Christian Kennedy, Kathy, Paul, Annie, Boo, Joshua, Laurie Kennedy, Peter Kennedy, Gabe Kennedy, Michelle (Skousen) Kennedy. Back row (l-r): Katrina, Brittany, unborn Sabrina, Jessica, Ben, Isaiah, Joe, Heidi, Tristan Taylor, Elisabeth, Kayla, Trisha (Skousen) Taylor, Wendy, Jacob, Sidney, Jen, Jackson.

PAUL B. SKOUSEN

Stuck in an ancient underground Roman chamber in central Israel, your intrepid author begs for *any* advice.

0 26575 50602 0